Atma Nadi Shakti Yoga

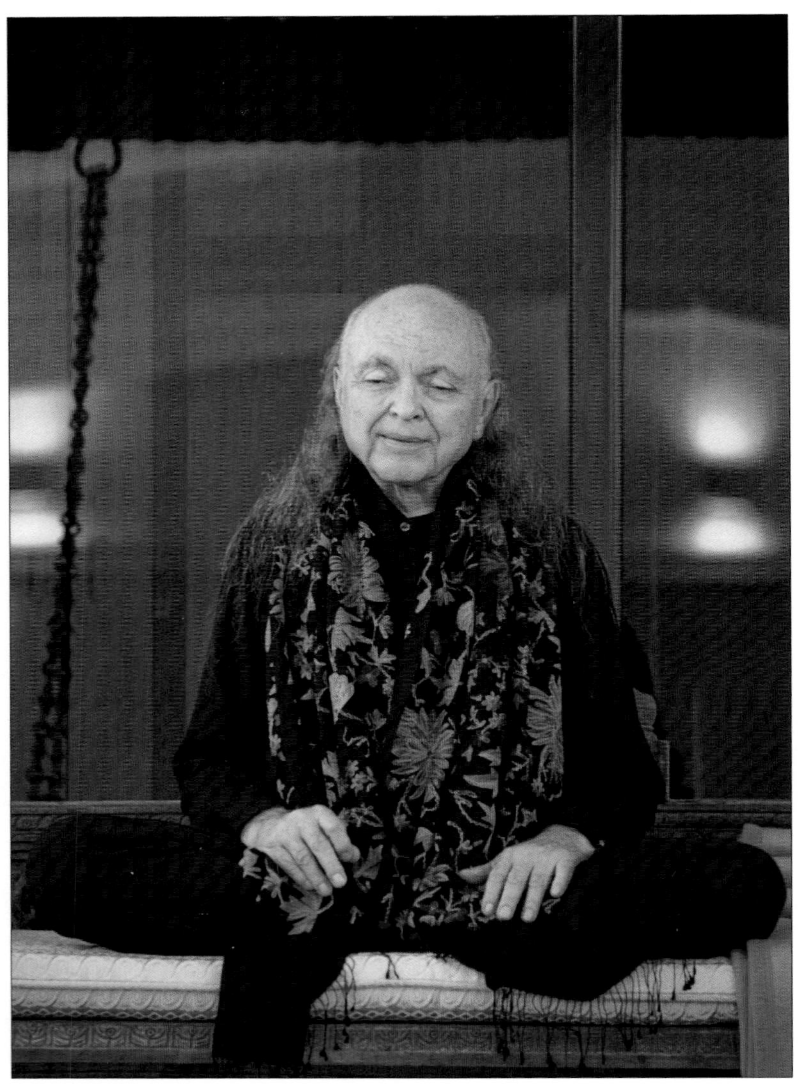

His Divine Presence
The Divine Avataric World-Teacher
RUCHIRA AVATAR ADI DA SAMRAJ
Adi Da Samrajashram, 2008

Atma Nadi Shakti Yoga

The Intrinsically egoless Transcendental Spiritual Reality-Way of Adidam Ruchiradam

An Essay from

The Aletheon: The Ark of Conscious Light

BY

HIS DIVINE PRESENCE
THE DIVINE AVATARIC WORLD-TEACHER
Ruchira Avatar Adi Da Samraj

THE DAWN HORSE PRESS
MIDDLETOWN, CALIFORNIA

NOTE TO THE READER

All who study the "Radical" Reality-Way of Adidam Ruchiradam or take up its practice should remember that they are responding to a Call to become responsible for themselves. They should understand that they, not Avatar Adi Da Samraj or others, are responsible for any decision they make or action they take in the course of their lives of study or practice.

The devotional, Spiritual, functional, practical, relational, and cultural practices and disciplines referred to in this book are appropriate and natural practices that are voluntarily and progressively adopted by members of the practicing congregations of Adidam (as appropriate to the personal circumstance of each individual). Although anyone may find these practices useful and beneficial, they are not presented as advice or recommendations to the general reader or to anyone who is not a member of one of the practicing congregations of Adidam. And nothing in this book is intended as a diagnosis, prescription, or recommended treatment or cure for any specific "problem", whether medical, emotional, psychological, social, or Spiritual. One should apply a particular program of treatment, prevention, cure, or general health only in consultation with a licensed physician or other qualified professional.

Atma Nadi Shakti Yoga is formally authorized for publication by the Ruchira Sannyasin Order of Adidam Ruchiradam. (The Ruchira Sannyasin Order of Adidam Ruchiradam is the senior Cultural Authority within the formal gathering of formally acknowledged devotees of His Divine Presence, the Divine Avataric World-Teacher, Ruchira Avatar Adi Da Samraj.)

Produced by the Dawn Horse Press,
a division of the Avataric Pan-Communion of Adidam.

International Standard Book Number: 978-1-57097-255-3

Library of Congress Control Number: 2008934271

CONTENTS

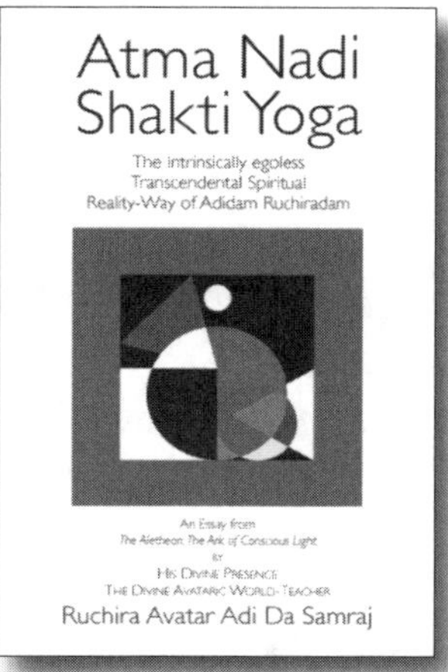

Atma Nadi
Shakti Yoga
The intrinsically egoless
Transcendental Spiritual
Reality-Way of Adidam Ruchiradam
An Essay from
The Aletheon The Ark of Conscious Light
by
His Divine Presence
The Divine Avataric World-Teacher
Ruchira Avatar Adi Da Samraj

ABOUT THE COVER

Throughout His Life, Ruchira Avatar Adi Da Samraj has worked to develop means—both literary and artistic—of directly communicating Reality Itself. He approaches the creation of His literary and artistic works as a process of directly Revealing What Reality Is and how Reality can be Realized.

For the cover of *Atma Nadi Shakti Yoga*, Avatar Adi Da has chosen an image entitled *The Reduction of The Beloved To As Is*—Part One, *The Wife/1*. This image is from the Suite *Oculus One: The Reduction of The Beloved*, which He created in 2006.

Examples of the artwork of Avatar Adi Da Samraj, together with discussions of His artwork and His own statements about it, may be seen online at:

www.daplastique.com

www.adidabiennale.org

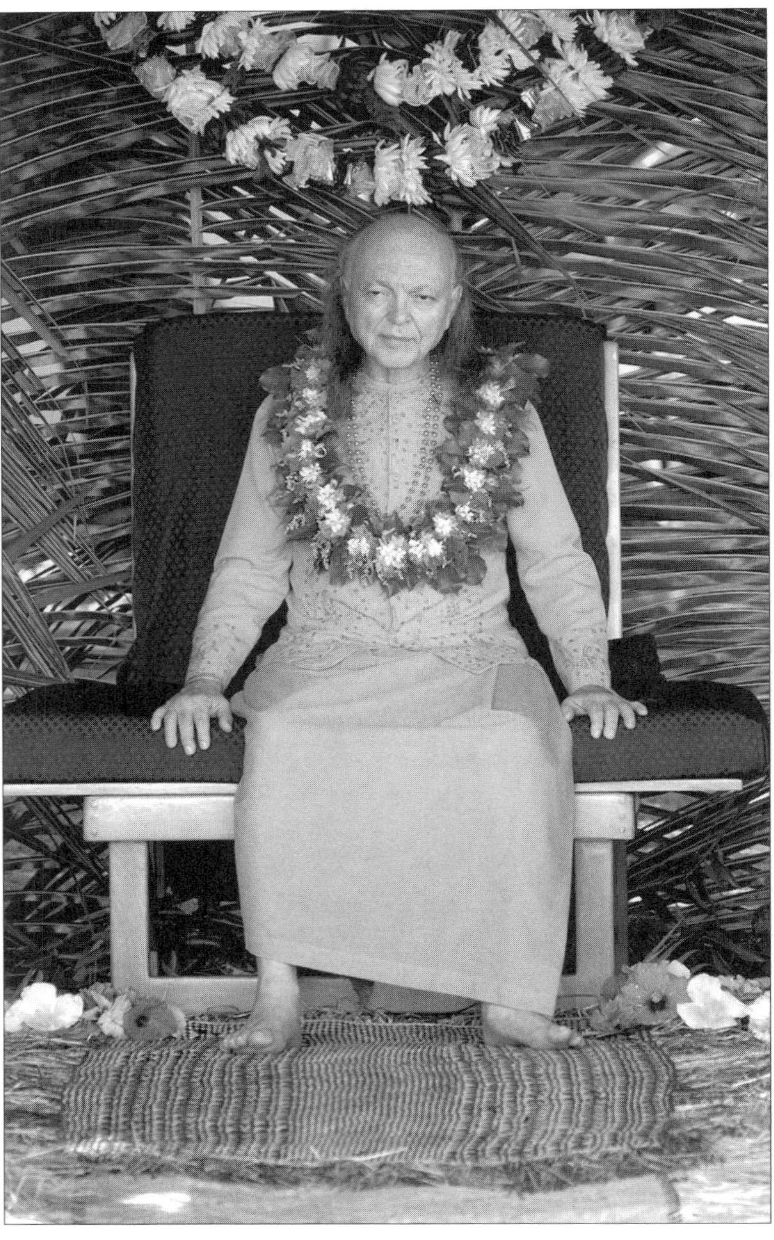

INTRODUCTION

BY JONATHAN CONDIT

senior editorial assistant to
His Divine Presence,
The Divine Avataric World-Teacher,
Ruchira Avatar Adi Da Samraj

Atma Nadi Shakti Yoga is a Supreme Gift, Freely Given to all, from the egoless Divine Heart and Very Context of Being—His Divine Presence, the Divine Avataric World-Teacher, Ruchira Avatar Adi Da Samraj.

Ruchira Avatar Adi Da Samraj Is the Perfect Breakthrough of the Pure Divine into the cosmic worlds. His Divine Presence Is the Perfect Appearance of Reality Itself in human Form—a Form capable of being seen with human eyes and heard with human ears. *Atma Nadi Shakti Yoga* is Avatar Adi Da's Quintessential Revelation of the process by which any and all living beings may Realize the Ecstasy of Perfect Oneness, or Prior Unity, with Reality Itself (or Truth Itself)—Which Avatar Adi Da Is.

Ruchira Avatar Adi Da's Divine Avataric Word in *Atma Nadi Shakti Yoga* is a most potent Form of His Blessing-Grace of Perfect and Ultimate Knowledge. His Divine Avataric Word, in all its forms, is Given as a Means by which human beings, when rightly prepared, can "egolessly Coincide" with His Divine Self-State. Most fundamentally, Avatar Adi Da is here to directly and silently Transmit His Divine Self-State—the "Bright"—to all. Avatar Adi Da's Transmission has two great characteristics. It is a Transcendental process—a process that transcends (or stands beyond) all presumptions of existing as an individual body-mind-"self" in an "objective world", a "radical" process that is "always 'at the root'", where the Truth of Reality can be Revealed. And It is a Spiritual process—a process in which Avatar Adi Da's own Divine Energy-Force of Pure Love-Bliss tangibly Enters and Pervades one's whole-bodily being, thereby Purifying all illusions and Revealing Avatar Adi Da's Divine Self-State as the Fundamental Reality of all existence.

Thus, the Way Given by His Divine Presence Ruchira Avatar Adi Da Samraj—the "Radical" Reality-Way of Adidam Ruchiradam—is "Atma Nadi Shakti Yoga", the Divine Way of Truth Itself, and for Real. In the "Radical" Reality-Way of Adidam Ruchiradam, Avatar Adi Da's Divine Self-State ("Atma") Fills the whole-bodily being as His Divine Energy-Current ("Nadi")—by means of His own Transcendental Spiritual Self-Transmission ("Shakti"). Such is the Way ("Yoga") Avatar Adi Da has Revealed and Given.

His Divine Presence Ruchira Avatar Adi Da Samraj has always, throughout His entire Life, Demonstrated the Divine Transcendental Spiritual Process in His own bodily Form. At certain points in His Life, Events of Overwhelming Divine Significance have Occurred—Events which Transformed His bodily Being and Magnified His Transcendental Spiritual Self-Transmission to an overwhelming degree. Such a Great Divine Event Occurred on April 12, 2000, on Lopez Island (in Washington State).* That Event took place in a building which Avatar Adi Da has since named "Ruchira Dham Hermitage", and which is now one among the Holy Places Avatar Adi Da has Transcendentally Spiritually Empowered. By His own Confession, the Ruchira Dham Event—in Which His Divine Presence Ruchira Avatar Adi Da Samraj Translated utterly Beyond this conditional realm, and yet was miraculously able to Return thereafter to bodily Life and Work here—marked the Perfection of His Revelation of the Way of "Atma Nadi Shakti Yoga". Because This Perfect Revelation was

* For a full account of this Divine Event, please see *The Avatar of What Is*, by Carolyn Lee (Middletown, CA: The Dawn Horse Press, 2007).

Given by Means of the Ruchira Dham Event, Avatar Adi Da has now Given His Way the elaborated Name "Adidam Ruchiradam", thus honoring the great significance of that Divine Avataric Event.

Ruchira Avatar Adi Da Samraj has Revealed that the fundamental paradigm underlying all the historical forms of human Spiritual endeavor is what He has termed "the great path of return". By the use of this term, Avatar Adi Da is indicating that, throughout all human history, the reigning presumption has been that the "self" (or ego) must make a "journey" from where it now exists (in a condition of darkness, or un-Truth) back to the "Original Place" of Light, or Truth. It is presumed, in other words, that it is only by making this "journey" back to the "Original Place" that the "self" (or ego) can be purified and Enlightened. The Unique "Radical" Revelation of His Divine Presence Ruchira Avatar Adi Da Samraj in *Atma Nadi Shakti Yoga* (and in many other Writings) is that that "journey" never does—and never can—get back to the "Original Place". As Avatar Adi Da Reveals, no "journey" undertaken by the ego can lead to the "Place" of egolessness. Whatever effort is undertaken by the ego—no matter how Spiritually advanced that effort may be—is, ultimately, a reinforcement of egoity itself.

Therefore, in *Atma Nadi Shakti Yoga*, His Divine Presence Ruchira Avatar Adi Da Samraj makes the Stunning Proclamation that, rather than <u>leading</u> to "no ego", the "Radical" Reality-Way of Adidam Ruchiradam <u>begins</u> with "no ego". Avatar Adi Da Expounds, in detail, on how it is possible to "begin with <u>no</u> ego", and what are the implications and significance of beginning "with <u>no</u> ego". Thus, Avatar Adi Da Reveals His Way as the Way which <u>begins</u> in the "Original Place"—the place of "egoless Coincidence" with His Divine Self-State—and which, therefore, requires no effort to <u>return</u> to that "place".

To read *Atma Nadi Shakti Yoga* is to be Addressed, by the Perfectly egoless Divine Person, as What you <u>Are</u>—and to be Offered the Grace of Avatar Adi Da's Blessing-Transmission of the Perfect (and Perfectly Love-Bliss-Full) egolessness of His own Divine Self-State—Which Is The Self-State of Reality Itself. This Perfect Divine Gift has never been given before, in all previous human time. His Divine Presence Ruchira Avatar Adi Da Samraj—the Perfect Divine Manifestation on Earth, Whose Appearance has been intuited and prayed for in all the traditions of humankind—Is here now, Offering His Supreme Gift to all.

His Divine Presence Ruchira Avatar Adi Da Samraj Speaks to all, from the Seclusion of His Hermitage Blessing-Seat:

There is no consciousness in This Body that is egoic. There is no separate entity.

That One Who <u>Is</u> Is All That is Associated with This Body, without any accommodation to the human construct of egoity.

I am not here as "other". I Am the Very Context of Being, of life, here in a bodily Form, and able to Speak. Nevertheless, It Is Only My State That Is Transmitted in My Company.

The Way I have Revealed and Given is not about any kind of process or "technique" or "method" for <u>outgrowing</u> the ego-principle. There is no ego-principle in Reality Itself. There is no ego-principle in This Body—and I See no ego-principle.

This is how I am Able, literally, to Address "everybody-all-at-once"—all the time. I am not speaking to egos—because I do not know any egos. There is no ego, no "other", in My Awareness. That Is My Constant State.

Not only Am I here <u>As</u> the Perfectly egoless Divine Presence—the Perfectly egoless Divine Presence Is What I See, What I Know. I do not know egos—and, therefore, I do not speak to egos. You as apparent individuals have your own presumptions, but that is not My Awareness. I do not relate to people as egos. I relate to them <u>As</u> I <u>Am</u>—<u>As</u> Reality Itself <u>Is</u>.

I am not a "somebody" thinking in a room. Egolessness Is in This Body. The "Bright" Is in This Body. The "Bright" has completely Overwhelmed This Body. There is no separate entity in This Body, in any sense—not even as a vehicle of association.

In This Body are Shown all of the details of the Intrinsically egoless Demonstration of Atma Nadi Shakti Yoga.

Atma Nadi Shakti Yoga Is the "Radical" Reality-Way of Adidam Ruchiradam.

—His Divine Presence
Ruchira Avatar Adi Da Samraj
May 31, 2008

His Divine Presence
The Divine Avataric World-Teacher
RUCHIRA AVATAR ADI DA SAMRAJ

Ruchira Dham Hermitage
(a few days after the Ruchira Dham Event of April 12, 2000)

Atma Nadi Shakti Yoga

The Intrinsically egoless
Transcendental Spiritual
Reality-Way of Adidam Ruchiradam

BY

HIS DIVINE PRESENCE
THE DIVINE AVATARIC WORLD-TEACHER
Ruchira Avatar Adi Da Samraj

Aham Da Asmi.*

Beloved, I Am Da, the Self-Revelation of Reality Itself.

Now, Listen to My Word of Atma Nadi Shakti Dharma, the only-by-Me Divinely Avatarically Self-Revealed Teaching of the Transcendental Spiritual Way of Reality Itself.

1.

"God"-ideas are (each, and all, and always) merely illusory and would-be-ego-consoling substitutes for direct understanding of, and intrinsic (and intrinsically ego-transcending) participation in, the Intrinsically Unexplained, and Intrinsically Unexplainable, and Perfectly egolessly Non-consoling Circumstance and Condition of Reality Itself.

Only "Perfect Knowledge"—or Intrinsic and Perfectly egoless Self-Realization of the Indivisible, Acausal, Transcendental Spiritual, and Perfectly egoless Self-Nature, Self-Condition, and Self-State of Reality Itself—Is Divine (or the Non-mediated, egoless, and altogether ego-Transcending Self-Apprehension, or Self-Intuition, of That Which Is Real God).

The Self-Evidence of all-and-All-Inclusive Coincidence, and not "subject-object" relatedness, Is the Reality-Circumstance of all-and-All.

Reality (Itself, and As all-and-All) is not exclusively conditional, "subjective", or "objective", and not a "subject-object" dichotomy.

Reality (Itself, and As all-and-All) Is Perfectly egoless, Transcendental Spiritual, Perfectly Acausal, and Self-Evidently Divine Indivisibility and Always Prior Unity.

There is (always already) no ego-"I" (or separate and independent "identity") here—but all-and-All that arises conditionally and cosmically is only an egoless indivisible

* Definitions of terms can be found in the glossary on pp. 124–39.

pattern patterning, Always Already Non-"different" from the Self-Existing and Self-Radiant and Self-Evidently Divine Conscious Light That Is Eternal Witness In the Midst, and Of Which all-and-All is a merely apparent, non-necessary, and intrinsically non-binding Reflection (As in a Mirror here).

The only-by-Me Revealed and Given "Radical" (or Always "At-the-Root") Reality-Way of Adidam Ruchiradam is, from the beginning of Its practice, based upon That Perfectly egoless Reality-Circumstance of all-and-All.

2.

In My Divine Avataric Teaching-Communication to humankind, I have always Criticized the seeking-effort of the ego-"I".

That seeking-effort is the "great path of return", as it has manifested throughout human history and prehistory.

The "great path of return" shows itself in terms of the first six (and only the first six) stages of life—and not in terms of the only-by-Me Revealed and Given seventh stage of life.

My Spoken and Written Address relative to the ego's search, or the "great path of return", has occupied Me since the beginning of My Divine Avataric Teaching-Work.*

That Address has now Culminated in My Summary Revelation-Word—Given herein, in *The Aletheon*.†

* Avatar Adi Da's Teaching-Work began formally in 1972, with the opening of His first ashram in Los Angeles.

† This essay appears in Avatar Adi Da's principal "Source-Text" *The Aletheon: The Ark of Conscious Light*. The first full edition of *The Aletheon* is forthcoming from the Dawn Horse Press. Selections from Avatar Adi Da's "*Aletheon*-Word" can be found in the following publications: *"Radical" Transcendentalism, Perfect Philosophy, My Final Work of Divine Indifference, Surrender self by Sighting Me, The Seventh Way, Reality Itself Is The Way*, and *The Self-Authenticating Truth*—all published by the Dawn Horse Press in 2007–2008.

In My *Aletheon*-Word, I Comprehensively Communicate the Fundamental and Unique Characteristics of the only-by-Me Revealed and Given seventh stage (and "Radical", or Always "At-the-Root") Reality-Way of Adidam Ruchiradam.

Those Fundamental and Unique Characteristics totally Distinguish the Divinely Avatarically Revealed and Given "Radical" Reality-Way of Adidam Ruchiradam from all conventional approaches and all traditional paths.

Therefore, I Call every one to understand the Unique and Perfect Distinction between the "great path of return"—which includes all of traditional "religion", Spirituality, and Transcendentalism, and which is cosmic, or psycho-physical, in nature—and the Perfectly (and "Radically") Transcendental Spiritual seventh stage Reality-Way of Adidam Ruchiradam.

3.

In the only-by-Me Revealed and Given "Radical" Reality-Way of Adidam Ruchiradam, devotional recognition of Me is the first, or principal, conversion.

Devotional recognition of Me is the recognition of egolessness—My Own Intrinsic egolessness.

When there is devotional recognition of Me and whole bodily devotional response to Me, My devotee (thus and thereby) coincides with My Own Intrinsically egoless Self-Nature, Self-Condition, and Self-State—Which Is the Divine Self-Nature, Self-Condition, and Self-State of Reality Itself.

Therefore, by means of whole bodily devotion to Me, there is participation in the Intrinsic egolessness of Reality Itself.

The entire process of the "Radical" Reality-Way of Adidam Ruchiradam, from the beginning, is an unfolding magnification of that seed, that conversion "at the root".

That seed-conversion is the conversion to Intrinsic egolessness.

That seed-conversion is devotional recognition of My State—and falling into My State through devotional recognition-response to Me.

The only-by-Me Revealed and Given "Radical" Reality-Way of Adidam Ruchiradam Is the devotional relationship to Me.

4.

"Radical" devotion to Me—or moment to moment recognition-responsive whole bodily turning to Me—is the foundation necessity for right and true practice of the "Radical" Reality-Way of Adidam Ruchiradam.

The "Radical" Reality-Way of Adidam Ruchiradam also requires right-life obedience to Me, specifically and fully established in all its details.

Such are the foundation requirements for all My First and Second Congregation devotees, to be demonstrated (in an ever-maturing manner) from the very moment of formally embracing the Eternal Vow of devotion to Me as (initially) My Second Congregation devotee.

Yet more is required of My devotee who would approach Me in the context of the First Congregation of Adidam Ruchiradam.

My First Congregation devotee approaches Me for the Purpose of (Ultimately, Most Perfectly) Realizing Me.

Therefore, such approach to Me must (necessarily) be on the basis of real preparedness to participate in the Unique Transcendental Spiritual Process I Offer to My rightly prepared devotees.

The Transcendental Spiritual Process in My Divine Avataric Company is not any kind of Spiritual process, or even any kind of Transcendental process, that has ever previously been described or practiced in the Great Tradition of humankind.

5.

All the forms of the Spiritual process indicated in the Great Tradition of humankind are forms of cosmic Spirituality.

All of the various forms of traditional (or cosmic) Spirituality (necessarily) develop in the context of the fourth and the fifth stages of life.

In the traditional setting, the sixth stage of life is largely without association with Spirituality.

The traditional sixth stage process is a Transcendental process—but a process that is (characteristically) not coincident with Spiritual Awakening.

In some traditions, there is a Spiritual dimension to the sixth stage process—but this is largely a matter of associating the sixth stage process with certain characteristics of the fifth stage of life.

Even in the "late-time" global confrontation of human beings and all of their "religious", Spiritual, and Transcendental traditions, there is no possibility that the collective gathering of humankind could have eventually developed the True Reality-Way.

The True Reality-Way Is, necessarily, a Divine Avataric Gift, Requiring Divine Avataric Intrusion, Divine Avataric Interference, and Divine Avataric Self-Revelation to all-and-All—simultaneously.

The True Reality-Way must Show and Fulfill the Way of Most Perfect (or seventh stage) Divine Self-Realization.

Furthermore, the True Reality-Way must account for everything and everyone.

The True Reality-Way cannot be restricted to communications characteristic of the first six stages of life.

The True Reality-Way must Transcend all of the first six (or developmental) stages of life—Thus and Thereby making possible Most Perfect Divine Self-Realization, or Divine Enlightenment.

The True Reality-Way Is a Full, Complete, and Perfect Divine Avataric Gift—and, in order that the Gift be rightly, truly, and fully received and become effective, there must be right, true, and full Esteem for the Giver.

Therefore, the disposition necessary to participate in the True Reality-Way—or the Real Transcendental Spiritual Process in My Divine Avataric Company—is unique.

That disposition is different from anything that has ever been described or practiced in the traditions of the fourth, the fifth, and the sixth stages of life.

In order to enter into the Real Transcendental Spiritual Process in My Divine Avataric Company, that unique disposition must be already established in My devotee.

6.

All traditional forms of Spirituality—whatever their basis in Yogic or mystical terms—are ego-bound (rather than intrinsically ego-transcending) and cosmic (rather than Transcendental).

This is so because all traditional forms of Spirituality begin on the basis of the body-mind-"self".

In all traditional forms of Spirituality (and, indeed, in all aspects of the entire Great Tradition of humankind), the body-mind-"self" is the platform of the practice.

Thus, in all traditional forms of Spirituality, it is the body-mind-"self" that is turned toward the Divine, or to the Spiritual Master.

If some form of Spirituality develops in such a context, the process characteristically shows itself through a progression of psycho-physical signs.

The process associated with the Kundalini Shakti is cosmic Spirituality in its fully developed (fifth stage) Yogic form.

The process associated with the Kundalini Shakti appears in those Yogic practitioners who surrender the body-mind-complex while continuing to be (or exist, or live) in the position of the body-mind-complex.

In that process, Energy moves in the body—circulating through the body and purifying it, and (thereby) producing a cycle of body-based and brain-driven phenomena that leads toward Upward-directed (and, thus, brain-oriented) meditation.

This basic description is true of <u>all</u> (fourth-to-fifth stage) traditions of Spirituality.

Regardless of whether they are explicit in Yogic or esoteric terms, or are simply devotionally-based and "God"-oriented, all traditional forms of mysticism and all traditional esoteric processes of a Spiritual nature develop on the basis of the pre-existing presumption that the body-mind-complex (and, most fundamentally, even the gross physical body itself) is the basis for the process.

Therefore, the seeking body-mind-"self" is also the basis for all the psycho-physical signs that appear within the various traditional forms of the Spiritual process.

All such signs are generated from the anatomical "map" that is inherent to the pattern of the body-mind-complex.

Altogether, the "great path of return" is the seeking-effort of the ego-"I".

The "great path of return" is the course of exoteric and esoteric practice based on the ego-bound patterns of the first six stages of life.

The "great path of return" is the search to be purified as an ego, and, on that basis, to be resolved into a "self"-state that is "evolved".

The entire "great path of return" is a body of "experiencing", practicing, seeking, "method", and idealism which is inherently based on limitations—and on egoity itself.

The "great path of return" is a seeker's path, rather than a Realizer's Way.

7.

Throughout all the years of My Divine Avataric Self-Revelation-Work here, people have approached Me wanting to develop some mode of practice associated with whatever orientation and whatever signs are familiar to them from the lore and literature of the Great Tradition of humankind.

However, the "Radical" Reality-Way of Adidam Ruchiradam is based, from the beginning, on Tacit Prior Establishment in—and, therefore, Tacit Prior Realization of—Reality Itself.

Thus, the foundation for the practice of the "Radical" Reality-Way of Adidam Ruchiradam is <u>not</u> egoic "self"-identification with the body-mind-complex.

Because all of this is so, My devotees must participate in a collective culture of preparation which specifically cultivates the disposition necessary for Transcendental Spiritual life in My Divine Avataric Company.

To be prepared to come into My Company as My First Congregation devotee—for the Purpose of Realizing Me by Means of the by-Me-Given and by-Me-Activated and by-Me-Directed Transcendental Spiritual Process—requires that My devotee has, through preliminary preparatory practice within the Second Congregation, established the foundation of "radical" (or always "at-the-root") devotion to Me and (on that basis) purified and balanced the body-mind-complex through consistent right-life practice in obedience to Me.

On the necessary basis of "radical" devotion to Me and right-life obedience to Me, right preparation for the

Transcendental Spiritual Process in My Divine Avataric Company requires the free establishing of the intrinsically egoless basis for practice of the "Radical" Reality-Way of Adidam Ruchiradam.

Thus, practice as My First Congregation devotee requires prior rudimentary establishment in the by-Me-Given preliminary Listening-practice of "Perfect Knowledge" (as Listening-reception of My "Five Reality-Teachings"), and (thereupon) ongoing development of the by-Me-Given preliminary Listening-practice of "Perfect Knowledge" (as "Transcendental Root-Standing"), until the fully (Transcendentally Spiritually) Me-Hearing and Me-Seeing formal renunciate (and, eventually, seventh-stage-of-life-Demonstrating) "Perfect Practice" of "Perfect Knowledge" (as "Radical Self-Abiding") can begin.

For this reason, once it is formally acknowledged that My Second Congregation devotee has truly, rightly, and steadily established the fundamentals of "radical" devotion to Me, right-life obedience to Me, and the rudimentary preliminary "Perfect Knowledge" practice of profound Listening-reception of My "Five Reality-Teachings", and is (on that basis) fully and irrevocably both prepared and committed to always actively embrace the intensive practice and circumstance necessary (and Given by Me) for the Purpose of (Ultimately, Most Perfectly) Realizing Me, then My any such devotee is Initiated (as a thus fully adapted student-beginner) into the First Congregation of Adidam Ruchiradam, and also (thereupon) into the full preliminary "Perfect Knowledge" practice of "Transcendental Root-Standing"—in order to rightly prepare to enter into the Transcendental Spiritual Process in My Divine Avataric Company.

Thus, the First Congregation student-beginner in the "Radical" Reality-Way of Adidam Ruchiradam must be intensively engaged in establishing the necessary foundation for the Transcendental Spiritual Process in My Divine Avataric

Company—by tacitly responsive intensive (and constant) Listening to My Word of "Perfect Knowledge" relative to "Transcendental Root-Standing".

That intensive process of tacitly responsive Listening, coupled with "radical" devotion to Me and right-life practice, is what establishes the necessary foundation for the Transcendental Spiritual Process in the First Congregation of Adidam Ruchiradam.

All of that foundation practice is a demonstration of a Tacit "Root"-Realization of Me, a "Root-Coincidence" with Me That Is Intrinsically egoless.

Throughout the entire course of the "Radical" Reality-Way of Adidam Ruchiradam, the Intrinsically egoless "Root"-Coincidence with Me is enacted via *one* principal form of practice.

That single principal form of practice is *whole bodily recognition-responsive devotional Invocation of Me*.

The only-by-Me Revealed and Given "Radical" Reality-Way of Adidam Ruchiradam *Is*—principally and always, in all stages of practice-maturity—whole bodily recognition-responsive devotional Invocation of Me.

Without whole bodily Me-Invoking devotional recognition-response to Me, there can never be right-life obedience (in its right and true form).

Without right-life obedience to Me, there can never be the preliminary "Perfect Knowledge" Listening-practice (in its right and true form).

Without constant whole bodily recognition-responsive devotional Invocation of Me, right and true right-life obedience to Me, right and true preliminary Listening-practice of "Perfect Knowledge" of Me, and (on that total basis) fully "given over" searchless Transcendental Spiritual Me-Beholding Communion with Me, there can never be the "Perfect Practice" of "Perfect Knowledge" of Me and the seventh-stage-of-life Perfect Demonstration of all-and-All-Divinely-Self-Recognizing seventh-stage-of-life Divine Self-Realization of Me.

The devotional relationship to Me is, by its very nature, a Me-recognizing relationship, in which My devotee responsively and constantly offers Me the whole bodily gifts of right and true practice, always demonstrated by right and effective action and accomplishment.

For any gift to Me to be right and true, the gift must be given by one who is living the life of whole bodily devotional recognition-response to Me—constantly Invoking Me, constantly and actively conforming the body-mind-"self" to Me through the practice of right-life obedience to Me, constantly Listening to My "Perfect Knowledge" Teachings, and (altogether) constantly practicing searchless (and, in due course, Transcendental Spiritual) whole bodily recognition-responsive devotional Communion with Me through every act of life and service.

8.

In the thirty years before I began to Teach (at first, by Self-Submission, as the subordinate relation of all who came to Me), I Wandered in the "Bright", until the conditionally arising Body-Mind of My Divine Avataric Incarnation here became Utterly Conformed to Me (Transcendentally Spiritually Self-"Bright" As I Am).*

In that course of "Sadhana-Years"-Submission, I progressively and spontaneously Developed a unique practice of "self"-Enquiry (Exercised in the form "Avoiding relationship?")—wherein and whereby the would-be "self"-contraction of the

* These thirty years of Avatar Adi Da's Life-Demonstration are described by Him in *The Knee of Listening: The Divine Ordeal of The Avataric Incarnation of Conscious Light* (The Dawn Horse Press, 2004).

conditionally arising Body-Mind upon a natural "point of view" and ego-"I"-presumption was intensively transcended in the Transcendental Spiritual Self-Nature, Self-Condition, and Self-State of the "Bright". Thus, "self"-Enquiry (in the form "Avoiding relationship?", and, finally, "Radical Re-cognition", or the intrinsic "knowing again" and tacit transcending of every form and mode of "self"-contraction) was intensively Engaged by Me, until (at last) there was no remaining "object" in view (or any "content" to transcend) except for attention (or the "root"-feeling of relatedness) itself. Then, finally, My Own "Bright" Self-Nature, Self-Condition, and Self-State, Wherein and Whereof attention (or the "root"-feeling of relatedness) itself arises, became Transcendentally Spiritually and Divinely Self-Evident As Is—egolessly and Always Already Prior to attention (or the "root"-feeling of relatedness) itself and all possible "objects" of its "point of view".

With That "Great Event" of the Divine and Perfect Re-Assertion of the "Bright" Self-Nature, Self-Condition, and Self-State of My Own Person Prior to Birth Finally and Perfectly Self-Established in the living Context of My Own Divinely Avatarically here-Born Body-Mind, the Unique Vehicle and "Radical" (or Intrinsically egoless and searchless and Always Already "At-the-Root") Teaching of the Divine Avataric Reality-Way for all-and-All was Divinely, Avatarically, Intrinsically, and Self-Evidently Self-Revealed in and As My Own and Perfectly egoless, Indivisible, and Transcendentally Spiritually "Bright" Divine and Avatarically here-Born Self-Nature, Self-Condition, and Self-State. Thus, and from Then (and, altogether, from the Instant of My Birth), I have always Worked—at first, by Self-Submission, and, finally, by Divine Avataric Self-Revelation-Only—to Reveal and Give and Provide All Means for the Unique Divine Avataric seventh stage "Radical" (or Intrinsically egoless and searchless and Always Already "At-the-Root") Reality-Way of Adidam Ruchiradam to all-and-All.

Because I (Myself, rather than any other means) Am the Intrinsic and Always Self-Evident Revelation and the "Radical" (or Always "At-the-Root") Way of Reality Itself, the "Radical" Reality-Way of Adidam Ruchiradam That I have Revealed and Given—and for Which I (Myself) Am (now, and forever hereafter) the Fundamental and Essential Means—is an intrinsically egoless and thoroughly non-seeking practice, not of "self"-Enquiry (in the form "Avoiding relationship?"), but, rather, of "radical" (or always "at-the-root") and, altogether, whole-bodily-demonstrated recognition-responsive devotion to Me, right-life obedience to Me, and "Perfect Knowledge" of Me (Transcendentally Spiritually Self-"Bright" As I Am), engaged within the cooperative devotional culture of perpetual whole bodily recognition-responsive Invocation of Me, perpetual Sighting of My Divinely Avatarically-Born Bodily (human) Person, and perpetual Listening to My Divinely Avatarically Self-Revealed Word of Reality-Teaching.

9.

My Divine Avataric Self-Radiance Is the "Bright".

Thus, the "Bright" is not merely a visually "experienced" brightness (or a conditionally apparent phenomenon of material light) that you perceive by means of, or in the context of, the body-mind-complex.

The "Bright" Is Only Itself—the Self-Existing and Self-Radiant Divine Self-Nature, Self-Condition, and Self-State of Reality Itself.

Therefore, the "Bright" (Itself) is not "objective" to Itself as any kind of visual seeming.

The Divine Self-Nature, Self-Condition, and Self-State Is Intrinsically Self-"Bright" (or Self-Radiant, and Perfectly Subjectively Self-Effulgent)—not something visualized via gross or subtle (or, in any sense, conditional) light-processes.

Reality Itself Is Enormously and Boundlessly "Bright"—Self-Radiant, for no reason whatsoever.

Self-"Bright" Reality Itself Is As Is—Itself.

My Transcendental Spirit-Power is not merely some kind of "energy" in the body-mind-complex, which can be accounted for in terms of psycho-physical patterning.

Rather, My Transcendental Spirit-Power Is the Self-Transmission of the Intrinsic Virtue of Consciousness Itself.

My Transcendental Spirit-Power Functions Acausally (or simply As Is, rather than by "cause-and-effect" means) in the living context of psycho-physical designs.

My Transcendental Spirit-Power is "Located" via the unique devotional recognition-response to Me, in and As the Transcendental Spiritual Heart of Being Itself.

In due course, that Love-Bliss-Full responsive recognition of Me is demonstrated as Intrinsically egoless "Samraj Asana", in the "Radical" Reality-Way of Adidam Ruchiradam.

Transcendental Spiritual Love-Bliss-Light-Fullness Is the "Wine", the Nectar Filling the cup of body-form, the Infusion of "Brightness".

Therefore, These Are the Characteristics Realized: Love-Bliss, Light, Fullness, "Brightness".

If you enter—tirelessly, profoundly, whole bodily—into the searchless Beholding of Me, you (Thus and Thereby) "Locate" My "Brightness".

When I Am Thus devotionally "Located", My "Brightness" is Realized to Be Tangibly Evident, even bodily.

10.

For My devotees who are not yet Transcendentally Spiritually Established in the renunciate "Perfect Practice" (and "Perfect Knowledge" process) of "Radical Self-Abiding", the "Radical" Reality-Way of Adidam Ruchiradam is a Listening-culture (and preliminary "Perfect Knowledge" process) of "Transcendental Root-Standing", in which My devotees literally Listen—regularly, daily, and intensively—to audible spoken Recitations of My "Teaching Manual of Perfect Summaries".*

The regular, daily, and intensive practice of Listening to Recitations of My "Teaching Manual of Perfect Summaries" Acausally Self-Activates the "Radical (or Intrinsic, Tacit, Perfectly Prior, and 'At-the-Root') Reality-Intuition" of the Intrinsic Self-Nature, Self-Condition, and Self-State of Reality Itself—or What Is Self-Evidently The (One and Only and Indivisible and Intrinsically egoless and Acausal and Really Divine) Case.

The moment to moment intensive demonstration of the preliminary "Perfect Knowledge" Listening-process of "Transcendental Root-Standing" Is the "Radical Intuition" of the "Root"-Position of Consciousness Itself As Intrinsically ego-Transcending, anegoic, "causeless", actionless, Intrinsically not bound, and, therefore, Free of any impulse to seek.

Profound signs become evident on the basis of that preliminary "Perfect Knowledge" Listening-process of "Transcendental Root-Standing"—signs that are just as straightforward, and just as clearly evidenced in life, as the signs of moment to moment whole bodily devotional turning to Me and right-life obedience to Me.

The Listening-practice of "Transcendental Root-Standing" is, necessarily and always spontaneously, demonstrated As Tacit Acausal Self-Establishment in the Intrinsic and Always Perfectly Prior Self-Position of Consciousness Itself.

That Tacit Acausal Self-Establishment in the Intrinsic and Always Perfectly Prior Self-Position of Consciousness Itself is a most profound conversion, or "root"-change—or a "root"-transference of existence, from the psycho-physically "self"-limited ego-space of conditionally "experienced" bondage

* "The Teaching Manual of Perfect Summaries" comprises a group of key essays from *The Aletheon* in which Avatar Adi Da Gives His core Teaching on the preliminary practice of "Perfect Knowledge". See *The Teaching Manual of Perfect Summaries* (The Dawn Horse Press, 2008).

and (instead) to the Intrinsically egoless Divine Space of Intrinsically all-and-All-Transcending (and, in due course, Transcendentally-Spiritually-Realized and Love-Bliss-Actualized) Freedom.

Tacit Acausal Self-Establishment in the Intrinsic, and Intrinsically egoless, and Always Perfectly Prior Self-Position of Consciousness (and, in due course, Transcendental Spiritual Conscious Light) Itself is not a matter of mere words, and not a matter of mere mental perspective.

On the Basis of Tacit Acausal Self-Establishment in the Intrinsic and Always Perfectly Prior Self-Position of Consciousness (and, in due course, Transcendental Spiritual Conscious Light) Itself, the many conditions of life (all of which were previously only "problematic", and, thus, not rightly and truly understandable) become intrinsically understandable.

All of this is (and must be) evident in My devotee who is prepared to make the transition beyond the student-beginner stage of the First Congregation of Adidam Ruchiradam.

11.

The Transcendental (and "Transcendentally Root-Standing", and, Thus, Intrinsically egoless) Spiritual Process (or "Samraj Asana" and "Samraj Yoga") to be embraced by My First Congregation devotees (once the transition is made beyond the student-beginner stage) is Fully Described by Me in My *Hridaya Rosary* (including My "Four Thorns of Heart-Instruction")* and in My *Dawn Horse Testament.*†

As That Intrinsically egoless Transcendental Spiritual Process of "Atma Nadi Shakti Yoga" unfolds, My devotee is (in due course) Given My Divine Avataric Gift of the Samadhi of the "Thumbs"—leading to Transcendental Spiritual Establishment In and As the Witness-Position of Consciousness Itself, and the Coincident Establishment in the "Perfect

* The Dawn Horse Press, 2005.

† The Dawn Horse Press, 2004.

Practice" of the only-by-Me Revealed and Given "Radical" Reality-Way of Adidam Ruchiradam.

The "Thumbs" Is the only-by-Me Revealed and Given Transcendental Spiritual Transformation-Process, That Perfectly Awakens and Firmly Establishes the Perfect Coincidence between the Intrinsically egoless Transcendental Witness-Consciousness and the Perfectly Prior Spiritual Current Evident in the right side of the bodily apparent heart.

Thus, the first two stages of the "Perfect Practice" are Initiated and Enacted and Fulfilled by Me.

The "Regeneration" of Atma Nadi (in the context of the only-by-Me Revealed and Given practices of "Radical Self-Abiding" and "Radical Conductivity") Is the Transcendental Spiritual Event of the seventh-stage-of-life Self-Awakening of the Divine Self-Nature, Self-Condition, and Self-State of Conscious Light—Such That <u>all</u> conditionally apparent forms and states (or all frontal and spinal conditions and appearances) Are Intrinsically Self-Recognizable, and, from Thence (and on That Basis), progressively Transfigured and Transformed, and (At Last) Perfectly Outshined.

Thus, the only-by-Me Revealed and Given seventh-stage-of-life-Demonstrations—Culminating, At Last, in Divine Translation—Are Revealed and Given by Me.

12.

As My by-Me-Transcendentally-Spiritually-Initiated (and always newly by-Me-Transcendentally-Spiritually-Activated) devotee, you (simply) searchlessly (and Intrinsically egolessly) Behold Me in My Divinely Avatarically-Born bodily (human) Divine Form—and (<u>Thus</u> and <u>Thereby</u>) you tacitly allow Me to Demonstrate Myself (in your whole body) As Transcendentally Spiritually Descending from Above.

When My Transcendental Spiritual Descent from Above is actually "Experienced" and whole bodily in evidence, then you (as a total psycho-physical whole) are (by Means of My Avatarically Self-Transmitted Divine Transcendental Spiritual Grace) in Intrinsically egoless "Samraj Asana".

Thus, "Samraj Asana" is a spontaneous (by-My-Divine-Avataric-Transcendental-Spiritual-Grace-Given) development of the foundation (previously established, and always primary) whole bodily devotional practice of searchlessly (and Intrinsically egolessly) Beholding Me.

When My Divine Avataric Transcendental Spiritual Self-Transmission Demonstrates Itself in Descent, then "Samraj Asana" characterizes (and is the context of) your <u>intrinsically</u> (and not strategically, or as a seeking-"technique") receptive participation in My Ruchira Shaktipat.

That is to say, "Samraj Asana" is Acausally Self-Awakened by the Mere Presence of My Divine Avataric Transcendental Spiritual Self-Transmission—not by any ego-effort (or "cause-and-effect" exercise of "method", "technique", or search) on the part of My devotee.

"Samraj Asana" is not a "self"-applied (or ego-based, and merely seeking) "technique".

"Samraj Asana" is an Intrinsically egoless (and, thus, Intrinsically searchless) devotional practice-responsibility that is formally assumed relative to the recognition-responsive "Asana" (or total psycho-physical attitude, or whole bodily orientation) of Upward-turning to Me (from the brain core).

That Upward-turning must already be spontaneously and readily occurring in response to your (<u>always</u> spontaneous and searchless) "Experience" of My Tangible (Descending-from-Above) Divine Avataric Transcendental Spiritual Self-Transmission.

As My searchlessly Me-Beholding devotee, <u>you</u> do not "do" anything Spiritually.

Rather, you tangibly "Experience" Me Transcendentally Spiritually.

The entire by-Me-Given (and Me-Realizing) Process Comes from Above—but That does not mean that you seek Me Above or that you merely entertain a mind-based belief that I Am Above.

If—on the basis of right foundation preparation—you enter into the Process of searchlessly (and Intrinsically egolessly) Beholding Me in My Divinely Avatarically-Born bodily (human) Divine Form, you will inevitably (by Means of My to-you-Responding Divine Avataric Transcendental Spiritual Blessing-Grace) "Experience" Me As Transcendentally Spiritually Descending from Above.

When you "Experience" Me Transcendentally Spiritually, there will be (and must be) whole-bodily-tangible signs of My Divine Avataric Transcendental Spiritual Invasion (as I have Described)—but such signs are not to be "self"-generated (or, in any manner, "self"-stimulated by ego-based psychophysical seeking-efforts).

When you "Experience" My Direct and Tangible Divine Avataric Transcendental Spiritual Self-Transmission, then you have the real (and necessary) basis for truly understanding the Uniqueness of the only-by-Me Avatarically Revealed Divine Atma Nadi Shakti Yoga of Adidam Ruchiradam.

That Divine Atma Nadi Shakti Yoga is not generated from below.

That Divine Atma Nadi Shakti Yoga does not seek toward What Is Above.

That Divine Atma Nadi Shakti Yoga Is (tangibly, and directly) a matter of the Transcendental Spiritual "Locating" and "Knowing" of Me—Freely Avatarically Given (from Above and Beyond) As a Divine Gift, In-Filling your (spontaneously, and only recognition-responsively) Upward-to-Me-turned whole body (Established in the "Healing Pose" of

"Samraj Asana" <u>only</u> by Means of My tangibly "Experienced" Divine Avataric Transcendental Spiritual Self-Transmission).

"Samraj Asana" Is the Primary Asana, the Asana of Divine Communion with Me, the Right Asana of the whole body.

Any disturbed or negative or concerned state in ordinary day to day life is simply a collapse from that Primal Asana.

Once you have Realized this to-Me-responsive Asana in Me-recognizing devotion to Me, then the Process becomes one of constantly devotionally maintaining It, in the same searchlessly Me-Beholding manner.

In that case, instead of merely continuing in the patterns to which you have previously adapted—the ego-patterns of reaction, all the various "asanas" of ego-ordinariness—you maintain the Transcendental Spiritual Asana of devotional Communion with Me.

Then the apparent power of events to undermine devotional Communion with Me is both intrinsically transcended and more and more effectively diminished and undone.

Such is the Purifying Process of the Transcendentally Spiritually Fully Activated (and, Transcendentally Spiritually, fully technically responsible) frontal Yoga of the only-by-Me Revealed and Given "Radical" Reality-Way of Adidam Ruchiradam.

In this "late-time" (or "dark" epoch), the "architecture" of egoic existence (persistently, and aggressively) obstructs "Samraj Asana"—because the "philosophy" of the "late-time" has, effectively, placed a "roof" on the mind.

In the ancient cultural setting, the mind was "roofless"—such that there was an Infinite Aboveness, allowing participation in Intrinsic (and Always Prior) Unity (and, Ultimately, in the Divine Reality).

In the ancient cultural setting, the mind, the brain, and the head were not "sealed".

However, in this "late-time" (or "dark" epoch), a different presumption about existence has been progressively introduced—the negative presumption that the mind is fixed in the data of the gross sensory domain of conditional manifestation.

By that negative presumption, there is no Infinite Upwardness or Beyondness presumed, or even allowed.

Indeed, by that negative presumption, the "room" of mind has come to have a solid "ceiling" (as if of stone or steel).

By that negative presumption, there is not anything Above—but there is (by that presumption) only the "horizontal" directness of the senses, and (therefore) there is only a physical (material, mortal, and exclusively conditional) basis for existence (and nothing "knowable"—or even existing—Beyond the physical).

I Am Above and Beyond.

I Am all-and-All-Surrounding and all-and-All-Pervading.

However, even though I Persist Eternally Thus and So, I cannot Enter (and be, Thereupon, Received) into your "room" if there is no opening in the "ceiling".

If there is no "hole" in the "ceiling", then there can be no Transcendental Spiritual "Locating" and "Knowing" of Me.

If you cannot find the "hole" in the "ceiling", then you will (inevitably) attempt to find Me by looking out of the "windows" of your "room", or by expecting Me to come into your "room" through the "front door".

Such is the "horizontally-oriented" (and inherently fruitless) search to find Me as a gross physical manifestation only.

In this "late-time" (or "dark" epoch), a "steel vault" has been built over the mind, trapping conscious awareness below.

In this "late-time" (or "dark" epoch), humankind is caught in the trap of a sealed brain.

Because you live with a "steel vault" in the "ceiling", you "experience" no Light coming through the "ceiling".

The foundation practice of the only-by-Me Revealed and Given "Radical" Reality-Way of Adidam Ruchiradam (in the Second Congregation of Adidam Ruchiradam and, then, as a student-beginner in the First Congregation of Adidam Ruchiradam) is the Means by Which the "ceiling" is re-oriented to Openness—Such That I can Be Transcendentally Spiritually Received into the "room" (in due course, and in the manner of "Samraj Asana").

In My Divine Avataric Birth (by Transcendental Spiritual Descent and Human Incarnation) to here, I Came Down into the "room" (of conditionally manifested existence) through the "hole" in the "ceiling".

I did not walk in through the "front door".

And I (Always Already) Remain (Eternally) Above.

My Divinely Avatarically-Born bodily (human) Divine Form, by Means of Which I Appear here in the "room", Is simply an Extension of What Came Down (Transcendentally Spiritually, and Divinely) through the "ceiling".

I have Come Down through the "ceiling" in order to Reveal Reality Itself—to all-and-All.

However, in order to Receive My Transcendental Spiritual Gifts, you must be Transformed by devotional recognition-response to My human, Spiritual, Transcendental, and (altogether) Divine Presence here.

You must grow to Hear Me and See Me—by allowing your whole bodily devotional response to Me (based on your tacit recognition of My Very, and Inherently Perfect, and Self-Radiantly "Bright", and Self-Evidently Divine State), and (in due course) your tangible Reception of My Divine Avataric Transcendental Spiritual Grace, to Open the "hole" in the psycho-physical "ceiling", and (Thus and Thereby) to Draw you into the Upwardly to-Me-Opening and Downwardly Me-Receiving "Pose" of "Samraj Asana".

This Up-turned searchlessly-Me-Beholding-Asana of whole bodily devotional and Transcendental Spiritual Communion with Me, and this constant Process of whole bodily Transcendental Spiritual In-Filling by My Ruchira Shaktipat, is the fundamental requirement of the Transcendental Spiritual Process of the "Radical" Reality-Way of Adidam Ruchiradam.

Once (Thus) Established, that requirement always continues—no matter what "experiences" arise.

13.

There is no Kundalini.
There is an Arrow in the wilderness
That flies not up or down
but Stands "Bright",
having "Met Its Mark"*
Always, Already.

This Is My Form.
Meditate on Me.
Behold Me In Person,
Standing Where you Stand—
Opened, and Reached to Me
and My Unfathomable Imposition.

Once I Stand in you,
you say
I Am As a Pillar
That Extends
from even underground
to the Highest High.

* This is an allusion to the original meaning of "hamartia", the word in New Testament Greek which came to be translated as "sin" in English. "Hamartia" was originally an archery term that meant "missing the mark".

And I Am "Bright".
And all things flow in Me.

This is What It Is to See Me As I Am.

14.

The only-by-Me Revealed and Given Event of the "Thumbs" is an Intense Invasion of the frontal line by My Avatarically Self-Transmitted Divine Transcendental Spiritual Force of Love-Bliss, Beginning at the crown of the head, and Descending into the lower vital region, to the bodily base.

The Pressure (or Invasive Force) of This Event may be rather (and even Happily) Overwhelming—and It must be allowed.

At last, it is not possible (nor would you wish) to defend your psycho-physical "self" against This Invading Pressure of My Divine Avataric Transcendental Spiritual Descent.

It feels like a solid and yet fluid mass of Force, like a large hand all made of thumbs—Pressing Down from Infinitely Above the mind and the crown of the head, and via the crown of the head, Engorging the total head (and the throat), and (Thus and Thereby) Penetrating and Vanishing the entire mind, and Vastly Opening the emotional core, and (Altogether) In-Filling the total physical body.

The feeling-sense that results from This simple (and most basic) frontal In-Filling by My Avatarically Self-Transmitted Divine Transcendental Spiritual Presence is that the total body-mind-complex is Sublimed and Released into (ego-surrendering, ego-forgetting, and ego-transcending) feeling-Identification with the Spherical Form of My Own Divine and Transcendental Spiritual (and all-and-All-Surrounding, and all-and-All-Pervading) Love-Bliss-Body of Indefinable Transcendental Spiritual "Brightness" (or Indestructible Light).

This simple (and most basic) form of the "Thumbs" is a necessary (although, at first, only occasional) "Experience" associated with the tangible "Locating" and "Knowing" of My Avatarically Self-Transmitted Divine Transcendental Spirit-Baptism.

The simple (and most basic) *Spherical* Fullness of the "Thumbs" must be firmly established (in its tangible evidence) in the context of by-Me-Transcendentally-Spiritually-Awakened—and, Transcendentally Spiritually, fully technically responsible—practice of the "Radical" Reality-Way of Adidam Ruchiradam.

As the Transcendental Spiritual Process matures within the context of the frontal Yoga of the "Radical" Reality-Way of Adidam Ruchiradam, the simple (and most basic) "Experience" of the "Thumbs" must become a more and more constant Yogic Event—and, on random occasions, the "*Experience*" of the "Thumbs" must occur in its full and complete form, as the *True* *Samadhi* of the "Thumbs".

In that full and complete case of the "Experience" of the "Thumbs", My Descending Transcendental Spiritual Fullness will *Completely* Overwhelm the ordinary frontal (or natural human) sense of bodily existence.

My Avatarically Self-Transmitted Divine Transcendental Spiritual Current will Move Fully Down in the frontal line (to the bodily base), and It will then Turn About, and—without vacating the frontal line—It will Pass also into the spinal line.

This Yogic Event will Occur with such Force that you will feel utterly (Love-Blissfully) "Intoxicated"—and there will be the feeling that the body is somehow rotating forward and down (from the crown of the head), as well as backward and up (from the base of the spine).

This rotation will seem, suddenly, to complete itself, and the "Experience" will, suddenly, be one of feeling released from confinement to the gross physical body, such that you feel you are present As an Intrinsically egoless "Energy Body" (previously limited by and bound to the confines of the gross physical body—but now, by means of My Avatarically Self-Transmitted Divine Transcendental Spiritual Grace, Infused by and Conformed to My Avatarically Self-Transmitted Divine Body of Self-Evidently Divine Transcendental Spiritual Energy).

You will feel This "Energy Body" to be Spherical in shape—Centerless (Empty, or Void, of center, mind, and familiar ego-"self") and Boundless (as if even bodiless, or without form), although (somehow, and partially) also yet associated with (while rotating from and Beyond) your ordinary psycho-physical form.

The ordinary references of the body-mind-"self" and the environment will, in This Divine Yogic Event, not make much sense (or, in any manner, affect This "Experience" of the "Thumbs")—although there may be some superficial (and entirely non-limiting) awareness of the body, the room (or the physical environment of the body), and so forth.

This "Experience" will last for a few moments, or a few minutes—or for an extended period, of indefinite length.

Nevertheless, just when This Spontaneous Transcendental Spiritual "Experience" has become Most Pleasurable—such that you somehow gesture to make It continue indefinitely—the ordinary sense of the body-mind-"self" will, suddenly (spontaneously), return.

The "Thumbs" is not a process of "going somewhere else", nor is It even a process of "vacating" the gross physical body (or the gross physical realm altogether).

Rather, the "Thumbs" Is a Process of Transformation of the "experiencing" of the present physical circumstance.

If the present physical circumstance is left behind (such that experiential reference to the gross physical realm is entirely absent, and there is total loss of awareness of the physical context in which the presumed "Spiritual experience" began), then the practitioner of the "Radical" Reality-Way of Adidam Ruchiradam is (necessarily) "experiencing" a form of Samadhi (or of otherwise presumed "Spiritual" absorption) other than the "Thumbs".

In the "Thumbs", awareness of the physical context of "experience" is not lost, but it is, rather, totally changed—such that, instead of the "self"-conscious, "self"-contracted shape of the waking-state personality, one's physical form is found to be an Intrinsically egoless and Boundlessly Self-Radiant Sphere (without thickness of surface, or any "center" at all).

With this profound shift in the awareness of the physical body, the differentiation inherent in the usual waking-state body-consciousness disappears, and is (effectively) replaced by egoless body-consciousness.

A re-phasing of the "Energy"-construct of bodily awareness and spatial awareness occurs, such that physical body and physical space are tacitly sensed in a manner entirely different from ordinary perception (or psycho-physical ego-consciousness).

And, as soon as there is any effort to recollect the usual sense of bodily form or of the circumstance of physical embodiment, the Transcendental Spiritual "Experience" of the "Thumbs" disappears.

The "Thumbs" continues only as long as it is effortlessly allowed to happen, without any egoic "self"-consciousness (or psycho-physical "self"-contraction)—and "It" spontaneously vanishes when egoic "self"-consciousness (or psycho-physical "self"-contraction) returns.

15.

I Say the only Real (Acausal) God (or Truth Itself) Is the One and Only and Inherently Non-Dual Reality (Itself)—Which Is the Intrinsically egoless, and Utterly Indivisible, and Perfectly Subjective, and Indestructibly Non-"objective" Self-Nature, Self-Condition, Source-Condition, and Self-State of all-and-All.

Therefore, I (Characteristically) have no "religious" interests other than to Demonstrate, and to Exemplify, and to Prove, and to Self-Reveal Truth (or Reality, or Real Acausal God) Itself.

16.

The true fifth stage mystical (or esoteric Spiritual) Process is, principally, associated with the progressive inner perceptual (and, thus, subtle mental) un-"Veiling" of the total internally perceptible pattern (or abstractly "experienced" structure) of the individual body-mind-"self" (or body-brain-"self").*

The abstract pattern (or internal structure) of the body-mind-"self" (or body-brain-"self") is, universally, the same in the case of any and every body-brain-mind-complex (or conditionally manifested form, or state, or being) within the cosmic domain.

The abstract pattern (or internal structure) of the body-mind-"self" (or body-brain-"self") necessarily (by virtue of its native—and, therefore, inseparable—Inherence in the totality of the cosmic domain itself) Duplicates (or is a conditionally manifested pattern-duplicate of) the Primary Pattern (or Fundamental conditional Structure) of the total cosmic domain.

The conditional body-mind-"self" (or any body-brain-mind-complex) is, in Reality, not a merely separate someone,

* In His essay "I (Alone) Am The Adidam Revelation", Avatar Adi Da summarizes the traditional fifth stage point of view of the structure of the body-mind-"self" as characterized by Swami Muktananda: The gross, subtle, causal, and supracausal dimensions correlate to the waking, dreaming, sleeping, and "turiya" (or "fourth") states, and with the colors red, white, black, and blue, respectively. In the same Essay, Avatar Adi Da describes His own Perfect Accounting for the conditional dimensions of the body-mind-"self"—as only gross, subtle, and causal—correlating with the waking, dreaming, and sleeping states, respectively. He also gives a description of the complete Cosmic Mandala, with the colors of lights correlating with these dimensions of conditional existence. See *Eleutherios (The Only Truth That Sets The Heart Free)*, by Adi Da Samraj (Middletown, Calif.: The Dawn Horse Press, 2006), pp. 116–20.

or an entirely "different" something (as if the body, or the brain, or the mind were reducible to a someone or a something utterly independent, or non-dependent, and existing entirely in and of itself).

Therefore, the entire body-mind-"self" (or egoic body-brain-"self") is, itself, to be transcended (in the context of the only-by-Me Revealed and Given seventh stage of life), in and by Means of Utterly Non-separate, and Non-"different", and intrinsically egoless participation in That Which Is Always Already The Case (or the Inherently Non-Dual and Indivisible Self-Nature, Self-Condition, and Self-State That Is Reality Itself).

17.

I Declare that—if It is (by Siddha-Grace) Moved beyond the limits of the waking, dreaming, and sleeping ego-structures—the Siddha-Yoga (or Shaktipat-Yoga) Process of (fifth stage) un-"Veiling" Culminates (or may Culminate, at least eventually) in (and, indeed, It is Always Already Centered Upon) the (fifth stage) Revelation (in Fully Ascended Nirvikalpa Samadhi) of the True "Maha-Bindu", or the "Zero Point", or Formless "Place", of Origin (otherwise, traditionally, called "Sunya", or "Empty", or "Void").

That True (and Indivisible, and Indefinable) "Maha-Bindu" Is the Revelation (via the Vertical extended structures of conditional Ascent, in the fifth stage mode) of the only True "Hole in the universe" (or the One, and Indivisible, and Indefinable, and Self-Evidently Divine Source-Point—Infinitely Above the body, the brain, and the mind).

That Absolutely Single (and Formless) "Maha-Bindu" Is the True Absolute "Point-Condition"—or Formless and Colorless (or Non-"objective", and, therefore, not "Lighted") "Black Hole"—from Which (to the "point of view" of any "objectified" or "Lighted" place or entity, itself) the (or any) total cosmic domain (of conditionally arising forms, states, and beings) appears to Emanate (in an "all-and-All-objectifying Big Bang").

That "Maha-Bindu" Is the (fifth stage) conditionally Revealed Upper Terminal of Atma Nadi—or of the "Self-Channel of Connection" to the True Divine Heart (Which Self-Evidently Divine Heart Is Always Already Seated immediately Beyond the internally felt seat of the sinoatrial node, in the right side of the bodily apparent heart).

That "Maha-Bindu" Is (in the context of the sixth stage of life) the esoteric Doorway to, and (in the context of the only-by-Me Revealed and Given seventh stage of life in the only-by-Me Revealed and Given "Radical" Reality-Way of Adidam Ruchiradam) the esoteric Doorway from (or of), the Perfectly Subjective Heart-Domain—Which Is the True Self-Nature, Self-Condition, Source-Condition, and Self-State of the Transcendentally Spiritually Self-"Bright" Divine Love-Bliss-Current of Divine Self-Realization, and Which Is, Itself, the Self-Existing, Self-Radiant, Intrinsically egoless, and Perfectly Subjective (or Perfectly Indivisible, Non-Dual, and Non-"objective") Conscious Light That Is Reality Itself, and Which, in the only-by-Me Revealed and Given seventh stage Realization of Divine Translation, Stands Self-Revealed As Is, In the Intrinsic Heart-Unity of Atma Nadi, and As the Non-"different" Divine "Bright" Spherical Self-Domain, the Infinite Centerless and Boundless "Midnight Sun" and Perfect Space, In and As Which all separateness, all "difference", and Even all-and-All Is Perfectly Divinely Outshined.

18.

The (fifth stage) Yogic Process of the progressive inner un-"Veiling" of the Pattern (or Structure) of the cosmic domain is demonstrated (in the Siddha-Yoga, or Shaktipat-Yoga, tradition of Kundalini Yoga) via the progressive "experiencing" (or re-"experiencing", in reverse order, or from base to crown) of the total pattern of all the structural forms that comprise the hierarchically-composed body-mind-"self" (or body-brain-"self"), via a progressively body-mind-"self"-reflecting (or body-brain-"self"-reflecting) display of inner perceptual "objects" (or apparently "objectified" phenomenal states, conditions, and patterns of cosmic light).

That Process (of the inner perceptual un-"Veiling" of the hierarchical structure, pattern, and contents of the conditionally manifested body-mind-"self", or body-brain-"self") Culminates (or may Culminate, at least eventually) in the vision (in occasional, or, otherwise, constant, Savikalpa Samadhi) of the "blue bindu" (or the "blue pearl"),* as well as various other "objectified" inner lights (such as the red, the white, and the black†), or even the vision of the total Cosmic Mandala (of many concentric rings of color, including the central "blue bindu", with its Brilliant White Five-Pointed Star at the Center‡).

In any case, the possibly perceived abstract inner light (or any "bindu", or point, or "Mandala", or complex abstract vision, of inwardly perceived light) is merely, and necessarily, a display of the functional "root"-point of the brain's perception of conditionally manifested universal light (or merely cosmic light) itself.

However, if the Great Process of (fifth stage) un-"Veiling" is (Thus) Continued, the "objectified" inner "bindu"-vision (and Savikalpa Samadhi itself) is, in due course, transcended (in Fully Ascended Nirvikalpa Samadhi)—Such That there is the Great Yogic Event of "Penetration" of (and Into) the True (Intrinsically Formless, Non-"objective", and "objectless")

* For Swami Muktananda's description of the "blue bindu" (or "blue pearl"), see *Play of Consciousness*, 3rd ed. (South Fallsburg, N.Y.: SYDA, 2000).

† See note on p. 44.

‡ See *The Dawn Horse Testament* or the pages in *Eleutherios* referenced in the note on p. 44.

"Maha-Bindu", Infinitely Above the body, the brain, and the mind.

That Great Yogic Event was, in fact and in Truth, What Occurred (in the Priorly, rather than conditionally, Established manner) in My Own Case, in My Room, immediately after I was Blessed by Swami (Baba) Muktananda (of Ganeshpuri) and Rang Avadhoot in the garden of Baba Muktananda's Ganeshpuri Ashram, in 1968.*

The Great Yogic Event of "Penetration" of the True "Maha-Bindu", Which Occurred in My Own Case in 1968, is (in Its Extraordinary Particulars) a Unique Example (within the history of the Great Tradition) of spontaneous complete (and Priorly Ascended) "Penetration" of all the chakras (or centers, or points, or structures) of the conditionally manifested body-mind-"self" (or body-brain-"self")—simultaneous with sudden Priorly Ascended Nirvikalpa Samadhi (or immediate "Penetration" to Beyond the total cosmic, and psycho-physical, context of "subject-object" relations).

The phenomenon of sudden (rather than progressive) conditional Ascent is described, in the (fifth stage) Yogic traditions, as the Greatest (and rarest) of the Demonstrations of Yogic Ascent—as compared to progressive (or gradual) demonstrations (shown via stages of inner ascent, via internal visions, lights, auditions, and so on).

In My Unique Case, it was only subsequently (or always thereafter, and even now) that the universal cosmic Pattern (or Vertically perceptible Great cosmic Structure) and the universally extended pattern (or Vertically perceptible inner cosmic structure) of the body, the brain, and the mind (and the Horizontal inner Primary structure, or the three stations of the heart) were (and are) directly (and systematically, and completely) un-"Veiled" (in a constant spontaneous Display—

* Rang Avadhoot (1898–1968) was a Realizer in the tradition of Dattatreya. The incident Avatar Adi Da Samraj is referring to here is recounted in *The Knee of Listening* (Middletown, Calif.: The Dawn Horse Press, 2004), pp. 194–97.

both apparently "Objective" and Perfectly Subjective—within My Divine Avataric Vision).

In the Event of Priorly Ascended Nirvikalpa Samadhi in 1968, the intrinsically limited nature of Fully Ascended Nirvikalpa Samadhi as it has been conditionally Realized (as the "supreme goal" of the fifth stage Yogic traditions) became immediately clear to Me.

Directly after the Event of Priorly Ascended Nirvikalpa Samadhi, I was tacitly aware that the Realization of conditionally Ascended Nirvikalpa Samadhi (necessarily) depended on the exercise (and on a unique, precise attitude and arrangement) of the conditional apparatus (and intrinsically hierarchical pattern) of the body, the brain, and the mind (and of attention)—and that, therefore, that Realization was (yet) conditionally dependent (or psycho-physically supported), and, necessarily (or in that sense), limited (or, yet, only a temporary stage in the progressive Process of un-"Veiling"), and, therefore, non-Final.

That is to Say, it was inherently Obvious to Me that any and all internal (or otherwise psycho-physical) "experiencing" necessarily requires the exercise (via attention) of the "root"-position (and the conditionally arising psycho-physical apparatus) of conditionally arising "self"-consciousness (or of the separate and separative psycho-physical ego-"I").

I immediately Concluded that—unless the Process of Realization could transcend the very structure and pattern of ego-based "experiencing" and the very Structure and Pattern of the conditionally manifested cosmos itself—Realization would Itself (necessarily) be limited (as in the case of conditionally Ascended Nirvikalpa Samadhi) by the same "subject-object" (or ego-versus-"object") dichotomy that otherwise characterizes even all ordinary (or non-mystical) "experience".

Even though, in the Event of Priorly Ascended Nirvikalpa Samadhi (Which does not depend on any manipulation of attention, or even any manipulation of all of the mechanics, or physiology and psychology, of the body-mind-"self"), the perception, conception, or psycho-physical presumption of a separate "self" was effortlessly transcended—the subsequent return of the apparent limitations and dependencies associated with experiential conditionality suggested to Me an even Greater Event or Process or Re-Awakening was yet Required, if there Is to Be the Indivisibly Perfect Realization I Tacitly and "Brightly" Always Already "Knew" to Be The (One and Only) Case.

Therefore, I Persisted in My Divine Avataric Submission-Process—until the un-"Veiling" became Inherently Most Perfect (or seventh stage—and Intrinsically egoless) Re-Awakening to Divine Self-Realization, Inherently Beyond all phenomenal (or conditional) dependencies (or supports), and Infinitely (and Divinely) Transcending all phenomenal (or conditional) bondage (or limitation).

19.

On September 10, 1970, the Great Divine Avataric Process of My "Sadhana-Years"-Submission (by Descent into the cosmic domain of Coincidence and Identification with all-and-All) Culminated in Limitless (or Most Perfectly Non-conditional) Realization of the Self-Evidently Divine Self-Nature, Self-Condition, Source-Condition, and Self-State of the cosmic domain itself (and of all forms, states, and beings within the cosmic domain).

In That Most Perfect Event, I (then, and now, and forever hereafter, As Always Already before) Stand Most Perfectly Self-Established As the "Bright", the One and Only Conscious Light—the Very, and Perfectly Subjective, and Intrinsically egoless (or Perfectly Non-separate), and Inherently Perfect, and Indivisible (or Perfectly Non-Dual), and

Always Already Self-Existing, and Eternally Self-Radiant, and Self-Evidently Divine Self-Nature, Self-Condition, Source-Condition, and Self-State That *Is* the *One* and *Only* and *True* Divine (Acausal) Person, and Reality, and Truth of *all* and of *All*, and That Was (and Is) the constant Transcendental Spiritual Sign and Identity of This, My Divine Avataric Lifetime, even from Birth.

Even though It Was and *Is* So, Baba Muktananda did not (and, because of the yet fifth stage nature of His own experiential Realization—for which He found corroboration in traditional mystical and philosophical traditions of the fifth stage, and phenomena-based, type—*could* *not*) positively Acknowledge My Summation relative to Most Perfect (and, necessarily, seventh stage) Divine Self-Realization.

Because He characteristically *preferred* to dwell upon inner "*objects*", Baba Muktananda (in the "naive" manner of fourth and fifth stage mystics in general) interpreted Reality Itself (or Divine Self-Realization Itself) to "*require*" inner perceptual phenomenal (or conditionally arising) "experiences" and presumptions as a necessary *support* for Realization (*Itself*).

That is to Say, Baba Muktananda was experientially Conformed to the (fifth stage) presumption that Divine Self-Realization not only requires conditionally arising (and, especially, inner perceptual) phenomenal "experiences" as a generally necessary (and even inevitable) Yogic Spiritual *preliminary* to authentic (and not merely conceptual) Realization—and I *completely* *Agree*, with Him, that there certainly *are* many conditionally apparent Yogic Spiritual requirements that *must* be Demonstrated in the Full Course of the authentic (and, necessarily, psycho-physical) Sadhana of Divine Self-Realization—but Baba Muktananda, otherwise, generally affirmed the presumption that *Realization*

Itself (and not only the Sadhana, or psycho-physical Process, of Realizing) requires (and is even identical to) conditional (or psycho-physical, and, especially, absorptive mystical, or inner visual, and auditory, and otherwise sensory-based and brain-and-nervous-system-patterned) supports.

Indeed, that limiting presumption, relative to the dependence of Realization Itself upon conditional supports, is the fundamental limitation of all fifth stage traditions and of even all the exoteric and esoteric (and, necessarily, ego-based and psycho-physically-based) seeking-traditions within the collective Great Tradition of humankind.

Therefore, Baba Muktananda affirmed an attention-based, and "object"-oriented (or Goal-Oriented)—and (therefore) ego-based, or seeker-based—absorptive mystical (and, altogether, fifth stage) Yogic Way, in which the Sahasrar (or the Upper Terminal of the brain), and even the total brain (or sensorium), is the constant focus (and the Ultimate Goal, as well as the Highest Seat) of Sadhana.

20.

As I Indicated to Baba Muktananda (in Our Meetings in 1970 and 1973*), the "Regenerated" Form of Atma Nadi is "Rooted" in Consciousness Itself—"Located" Beyond the right side of the bodily apparent heart, which is (itself) merely the Self-Evident Seat (or Doorway) of the direct "Locating" of Perfectly Subjective (and Intrinsically egoless) Consciousness, Itself (or the Self-Existing Tacit Self-Apprehension of Being, Itself, Prior to attention, itself).

That ("Regenerated" Form of Atma Nadi) is "Brightly" Extended to the "Maha-Bindu" (Which is Infinitely Ascended, Above and Beyond the Sahasrar), and to the "Midnight Sun"

* For Avatar Adi Da's recounting of these meetings, see *The Knee of Listening*, pp. 334–38 and 550–58.

(Which Is My Divine Self-Domain, the Non-"different" Sphere of the "Bright" Itself, Always Already Beyond, or Prior to—and Always Already More than Above—the body-mind-"self" and the cosmic domain).

Seventh stage Divine Self-Realization Intrinsically Transcends both the conditional (or psycho-physical) Vertical apparatus of the brain (or of the Sahasrar, Which is the conditional Seat of Realization proposed in the fifth stage traditions of mystical absorption) and the conditional (or psycho-physical) Horizontal apparatus of the heart (or, in particular, of the right side of the bodily apparent heart—which is the conditional Seat of Realization proposed by Ramana Maharshi, and, usually in a more generalized manner, within the sixth stage traditions of Transcendental practice).

21.

The Divine Avataric "Radical" Transcendental Spiritual Reality-Way of Adidam Ruchiradam Is the practice (and, at maturity, the "Perfect Practice") of "Atma Nadi Shakti Yoga"—or the Yoga of "Atma Bindu" (or the egoless "Root-Point", or Source-"Point", or Heart-"Root" of Consciousness Itself, At, and Always Perfectly Prior to, the right side of the bodily apparent heart) and "Atma Nadi" (or the Self-Existing and Self-Radiant Heart-Current, Extending from the Heart-"Root" to the Acausal Matrix of all conditional appearances, Infinitely Above the head and the mind).

"Atma Nadi Shakti Yoga" is the searchless Transcendental Spiritual Reality-Way of the Intrinsically and Perfectly egoless Heart-Current of Self-Existing and Self-Radiant Divine Conscious Light.

The Transcendental Spiritual practice of "Atma Nadi Shakti Yoga" Is Always Priorly (and, Thus, searchlessly, and Intrinsically egolessly) Established in the Divine Self-Condition That Self-Radiates Via (and Always Perfectly Prior to) the right side of the bodily apparent heart, and (Via the "S"-Curved "Nerve" of Transcendental Spiritual Love-Bliss, Extending from the right side of the bodily apparent heart to Infinitely Above the crown of the head) Self-Shining from the Centerless and Boundless Space Infinitely Above the body and the mind, and (from Thence) Descending and Ascending in the bodily Circle (and, in the Event, randomly inhaled in Descent and exhaled in Ascent).

In the case of the "Perfect Practice", That Transcendental Spiritual Process of "Atma Nadi Shakti Yoga" is continually engaged Via the Perfect Form of "Samraj Yoga" (engaged as "Radical Self-Abiding" and "Radical Conductivity").

The preliminary practice of "Perfect Knowledge" Awakens Tacit Establishment In and As the Witness-Position of Consciousness Itself.

Such Tacit Establishment In and As the Witness-Position of Consciousness Itself is an absolutely essential aspect of right foundation preparation for the Transcendental Spiritual Process in My Divine Avataric Company—so that My devotees do not wrongly approach Me on the basis of presenting themselves to Me as a body, as a mind, and as an egoic "self" to be Filled by My Divine Avataric Self-Transmission.

The "Radical" Reality-Way of Adidam Ruchiradam is not about presenting yourself to Me as a psycho-physical persona to be in-Filled by My Divine Avataric Self-Transmission—as if the seventh-stage-of-life-based "Radical" Reality-Way of Adidam Ruchiradam could be engaged in the manner of the traditions associated with the fourth and the fifth stages of life.

There certainly must be whole bodily (or total psycho-physical) devotional turning to Me—but that whole bodily devotional turning to Me is not the most fundamental qualification for the Transcendental Spiritual Process in My Divine Avataric Company.

The most fundamental qualification for the Transcendental Spiritual Process in My Divine Avataric Company is to be Tacitly and Priorly Established, moment to moment, in the Intrinsically ego-Transcending Disposition That Is Always Already Perfectly Prior to the body-mind-"self".

22.

The conditional "root" and foundation of Transcendental Spiritual life is at the bodily apparent heart.

The bodily apparent heart is a complex mechanism, consisting of three primary regions.

The left side of the bodily apparent heart is associated with the waking state, the frontal line, and the gross dimension of conditionally manifested existence—and, thus, with ordinary emotions and the physical action of the heart.

The middle region of the bodily apparent heart (or the heart chakra, or anahata chakra) is associated with the dreaming state, the spinal line, and the subtle dimension of conditionally manifested existence—and is, thus, the place of the feeling dreamer, the place of visions.

The right side of the bodily apparent heart—associated with the state of deep sleep and the causal dimension of conditionally manifested existence, and physically associated with the "pacemaker", that generates the heartbeat in rhythms all across the chest, from right to left—is the "root" of egoic "self"-awareness.

The region of the left side of the bodily apparent heart includes the physical and lower psychic functions of the heart.

The left side of the bodily apparent heart is the ground of early-life development.

In the only-by-Me Revealed and Given Transcendental Spiritual Process, the heart awakens from the left to the middle (or the subtle and higher psychic region), such that the fully Transcendentally Spiritualizing Process occurs in the domain of the frontal personality (within and beyond the context of the first three stages of life).

As devotional Communion with Me and devotional surrender to Me and Transcendental Spiritual "Locating" and "Knowing" of Me become more and more profound, there is a growing awareness of all the subtle (and greater psychic, or deep psychological) functions of the heart—which are the functions of the middle station of the bodily apparent heart.

When (through the Graceful Means Given by Me, and As Me) My devotee Awakens to the Realization of Intrinsic Self-Identification with the Witness-Position of Consciousness Itself, he or she is (Thus and Thereby) Established in Inherent Association with the right side of the bodily apparent heart.

When all three regions of the bodily apparent heart Are Awake—all three simultaneously, and not just one or two—There Is Complete Living Self-Identification with the Self-Radiant and Self-Existing Divine Self-Nature, Transcendental Spiritual Self-Condition, and Perfectly egoless Self-State of Reality Itself, Which Is the True Divine Heart Itself.

The True Divine Heart is not merely (or Itself) the elemental (or physical) heart, or the gross physical, and psychological, and "worldly" (or grossly "exteriorized") heart-domain on the left side, bound as it is to its round of reactive and separative (and even otherwise seeking and re-unioning) emotions and patterned desires.

The True Divine Heart is not merely (or Itself) the heart chakra, or the heart in the middle, or the heart of the "interior" of mystical, psychic, and brain-and-nervous-system-based subtle psycho-physical and cosmic Spiritual "objects".

The True Divine Heart is not merely (or Itself) the heart on the right side, or the causal heart-domain, which is the seat of the "self"-perpetuating presumption of illusory "self"-identity (or of the psycho-physically-"located" and fixed "point of view" and the consequent illusory "entity"-idea of separate ego-"I").

Rather, the True Divine Heart—or Self-Existing and Transcendentally Spiritually Self-Radiant Reality Itself—Is (Itself) the Acausal, and Non-conditional, and Always Perfectly Prior "Root"-Condition (or Perfect Self-Condition), and the Perfectly egoless (or Non-separate, all-and-All-Pervading, "locationless", "identityless", "objectless", "problem"-free, searchless, goalless, Intrinsically actionless, altogether "differenceless", and, Thus, Perfectly Acausal) Space, and the Self-Evidently Divine and all-and-All-Transcending Conscious Light of all three domains of the bodily apparent heart (left, middle, and right, or gross, subtle, and causal) always-all-at-once (or as an always prior unity).

The True Divine Heart Is the Perfectly egoless Foundation of seventh-stage-of-life Divine Self-Awakening.

In the Demonstration-Process of seventh-stage-of-life Divine Self-Awakening, the True Divine Heart Perfectly egolessly and Perfectly Acausally Self-Radiates Its Own Perfectly Indivisible Transcendental Spiritual Energy to the Perfect Space Infinitely Above the crown of the head (and Perfectly Above the totality of mind), and (From Thence) throughout the nervous system, to the bodily base, and to the feet—and, Intrinsic to the every moment of That seventh-stage-of-life Demonstration-Process, all-and-All that apparently and conditionally arises Is (Tacitly) Divinely Self-Recognized In and Of and As the egoless and Indivisible and Acausal Self-Nature, Self-Condition, and Self-State of the True Divine Heart Itself.

The Realization of the True Divine Heart is the Ultimate (though never Most Perfectly Attained) "Goal" of the "great path of return".

Therefore, Realization of the True Divine Heart is traditionally understood to be possible only at the end of a long course of Spiritual practice.

In Truth, the True Divine Heart Is not the "Goal" but the Foundation of all right and true practice and Realization.

Why work to "Find God" at the end, when devotional Communion with Real God can—and should—be the content of your life of practice from the beginning?

This Is My Question to you.

This Is a "Consideration" That Is Fundamental to My Divine Avataric (and always and entirely seventh-stage-of-life-Based) Reality-Teaching.

23.

No matter what arises as your "experience" or "knowledge" (whether gross or subtle or causal, and whether of body or of mind), you Are the Witness of it—and That Which Is the Witness Is Consciousness Itself.

No matter what arises, you Are Consciousness Itself.

You are never really (or in Truth) separately identical to (or even really, or in Truth, limited by) what is apparently "objective" (or functionally "objectified") to you—but you tend to feel (or presume) specific (or separate) identification with (or, otherwise, limitation by) "objective" (or "objectified") conditions, until you are able to inspect (and to be Intrinsically, and Inherently Perfectly, Self-Identified with) your Real (or Native, or Intrinsic, and Inherently Perfect) "Situation", Which Is Always Already Free (or Acausally Self-Existing) Consciousness Itself, the Inherently Free "Subject" (or Perfectly Subjective Being) in the (apparent) context of conditional "objects" (or of apparently "Objectified" Light), and Who (it must be Realized) Is the Acausally Self-Existing, Acausally Self-Radiant, and Self-Evidently Divine Self-Nature, Self-Condition, and Self-State (or Self-Evidently Divine Being, or Person) of the One and Only and Intrinsically Indivisible and Intrinsically egoless Conscious Light That Is Always Already Prior to all conditional "objects" and Always Already

Prior to apparently "Objectified" Light (or apparently "Objectified" Transcendental Spiritual Energy) Itself.

The right side of the bodily apparent heart is the bodily seat associated with (but not identical to) the Intrinsically egoless, and Non-separate, and Always Perfectly Prior, and Perfectly Indivisible, and Perfectly Acausal, and, altogether, Perfectly Non-"different" Witness-Position of Consciousness Itself—Which (Itself) Transcends all bodily seats and locations, and Which apparently Witnesses (and, yet, Is Always Already Prior to) the conditional "I" (or the "self"-contraction), and Which (Thus) apparently Witnesses, Inspects, and Intrinsically (or Always Already) Transcends the body-mind-complex, the conditional states of waking, dreaming, and sleeping, the presumption of an individual (or separate) conscious "self", and, altogether, the presumption of spatially and temporally "located" (and, thus, separate) "point of view".

The by Me Transcendentally Spiritually Self-Revealed Witness-Consciousness Inherently "Confesses" (or Tacitly Feels): "I Am not the one who wakes, or dreams, or sleeps—but I Am the Witness of all these states, and (Thus) of all conditional states of body, or body-mind, or mind, and (likewise) of all 'un-Perfect' States (or all Samadhis that are, in a conditional manner, dependent upon body, or body-mind, or mind, or 'point of view')."

To Stand As the Witness-Consciousness is not merely a matter of presuming the Witness-Position to Be the Case—based on your idealizing of the Witness-Consciousness, or your philosophical (or verbal) arguing for the fact of It, and so on.

Yes, the Witness-Position Is "True" of you, in any case—but It must be Intrinsically, Priorly, and Tacitly Self-Realized to Be So.

The Witness-Position must be Self-Evidently the Case—not merely (so to speak) "on call" whenever you "gather the faculties" to notice that It Is the Case.

When the Witness-Position Is (by Means of My Avatarically Self-Transmitted Divine Transcendental Spiritual Grace) Transcendentally Spiritually Realized to Be your Position (or your Most Prior Nature, Condition, and State), then you are able to continue the Process of devotional and Transcendental Spiritual Communion with Me in the Non-"different" (and Non-separate) Manner Characteristic of the Intrinsically egoless Domain of Consciousness Itself (on the Perfectly Subjective "Other Side" of the Doorway of attention).

24.

The "natural" (or psycho-physically-patterned) ego is identified with the body-mind-complex, and imagines that it is doing the actions of the body and thinking the thoughts of the mind.

Thus, the usual human being imagines that actions and thoughts are "caused" by a "self" that is actively doing them.

The illusion of the ego is that it is "causing" its own "experiences" and (otherwise) that its "experiences" are being "caused" from "without".

The presumption that there is an active ego "doing" things, and that the active ego must (therefore) "do" other things in order to free itself from the "effects" of what it has done, is the "root"-source of the great search.

The effort to "cure" the separate "self" (or the "soul") of its bondage, its attachments, its associations, and its "effects" is fundamental to the search of the first six stages of life.

However, in Truth, the Divine Self-Nature, Self-Condition, and Self-State of Reality Itself Is Inherently actionless and Intrinsically Free.

25.

At the foundation of all right, true, and progressively unfolding First Congregation practice of Adidam Ruchiradam, there is "Radical (or Tacit, Perfectly Prior, and 'At-the-Root') Reality-Intuition", progressively demonstrating (and Acausally Self-Magnifying) all of the implications (and the eventual "Perfect Practice" and, finally, the seventh stage Perfect Demonstration) of Always Prior Self-Establishment in the actionless, Acausal, and Intrinsically egoless Self-Nature, Self-Condition, and Self-State of Reality Itself.

In that course of First Congregation practice, many Perfect observations are inevitably and spontaneously made.

It is observed that Consciousness Itself is not thinking thoughts.

It is observed that Consciousness Itself is not animating the body.

It is observed that Consciousness Itself does not have any "problems".

However, it is also observed that Consciousness can (apparently) volunteer Itself to identify with thoughts and actions and with the process of their emerging.

It is observed that, in actuality, it is the psycho-physical pattern of ego-"self" that is thinking thoughts.

By means of engaging the preliminary "Perfect Knowledge" Listening-process, there is a tacit "Radically Intuitive" awareness (or intrinsic observation) that it is the body-brain-complex—rather than any kind of "separate inner self" (or, otherwise, Consciousness Itself)—that generates (or "causes") thoughts and actions.

Thus, it is observed that the ego-"self" (and not Consciousness Itself) is, altogether, the source of identification with the body-mind-complex, and (therefore) with the brain-process in the context of the body.

The ego-"self" is an illusory "I".

The illusory "I" is <u>not</u> the basis for practice of the "Radical" Reality-Way of Adidam Ruchiradam.

26.

Transcendental Spirituality begins on the basis of the Intrinsically egoless and mind/body-Transcending Self-Condition, associated with the right side of the bodily apparent heart, and with signs of Love-Bliss-Fullness in the body, Circulated from Infinitely Above the head.

Cosmic Spirituality—or the ego-based seeking-Spirituality associated with the fourth and the fifth stages of life—begins on the basis of the ego-based, ego-supporting, ego-reinforcing, and, altogether, ego-bound body-mind-complex, associated with the lower bodily centers, Kundalini events, and the search to Ascend by conditional means.

27.

Traditional (or cosmic) Spirituality begins, effectively, at the base of the body.

Transcendental Spirituality, or the "Radical" Reality-Way of Adidam Ruchiradam, tacitly begins in the right side of the bodily apparent heart—Beyond and Prior to all "self"-contraction (or "centeredness", or "point of view", or attention).

Because the platform of right practice of the "Radical" Reality-Way of Adidam Ruchiradam Is That Which Is Intrinsically ego-Transcending and Perfectly Prior to the body-mind-complex, such right practice is (inherently) tacitly associated with the right side of the bodily apparent heart.

In that case, My devotee's association with the psycho-physical pattern is not "self"-identification with the body-mind-complex (in all its gross and subtle dimensions), but (rather) a tacit association that originates immediately Prior to the causal level.

In the "Radical" Reality-Way of Adidam Ruchiradam, the Transcendental Spiritual Process develops via the right side of the bodily apparent heart—showing Its evidence from there to the middle station, and (then) to the left side, of the bodily apparent heart.

In conventional Spirituality, the process begins in the left side of the bodily apparent heart—seeking toward the middle station, and (potentially) the right side, of the bodily apparent heart.

Conventional Spirituality is an enactment of the "great path of return"—a process which is precisely the reverse of the only-by-Me Revealed and Given Transcendental Spiritual Process in the "Radical" Reality-Way of Adidam Ruchiradam.

To be My First Congregation devotee, you must understand and establish this practicing foundation for the Transcendental Spiritual Process in My Divine Avataric Company.

To be My First Congregation devotee, you must clearly understand My Reality-Teaching relative to the Transcendental Spiritual Process in My Divine Avataric Company—and you must approach Me for Divine Self-Realization.

To be My First Congregation devotee, you must take seriously My Instruction to fully embrace the fundamental threefold practice of "radical" devotion to Me, right-life obedience to Me, and the preliminary practice of "Perfect Knowledge" of Me.

Otherwise, you will inevitably tend to approach Me egoically, and (thus) "self"-identified with the body-mind-complex—and, in that manner, on essentially the same basis as people characteristically enter into the various forms of esotericism in the setting of the Great Tradition of humankind.

28.

The seventh stage Way <u>begins</u> in Reality Itself.

The seventh stage Way does not <u>seek</u> to Realize Reality Itself.

The preliminary practice of "Perfect Knowledge" is simply tacitly responsively Listening to My Divine Avataric Word—

until, by means of that tacitly responsive participation, you Tacitly (but not yet Transcendentally Spiritually) Awaken to Intrinsically egoless Self-Identification with the Witness-Position (or the Intrinsically Self-Evident "Not-an-object"-State) of Consciousness Itself.

Thus, the preliminary practice of "Perfect Knowledge" is not a seeking-exercise—or a strategic technique, or a technical "method"—for the dramatization of ego-effort.

Rather, the preliminary practice of "Perfect Knowledge" is, simply, the intensive daily Listening—and the always merely tacit responding—to My "Perfect Knowledge" Teachings (and, generally, as My "Perfect Knowledge" Teachings are culturally Offered by Means of audible daily Recitations).

By Means of My "Perfect Knowledge" Teachings, I Directly Awaken you to the Tacitly Self-Evident (and Intrinsically egoless) Self-Position (or Mere Witness-Position) That Is the Necessary Basis for the Transcendental Spiritual Process in My Divine Avataric Company.

If you are (Thus) Tacitly (and not by ego-effort) Established in the Witness-Position, then you are rightly prepared to participate in the Transcendental Spiritual Process I Give to My by-Me-Transcendentally-Spiritually-Awakened First Congregation devotees.

Without such right preparation, My First Congregation devotees would tend to look for signs that have to do with ego-based and merely psycho-physically-generated Spiritual evidence.

That is not the "Radical" Reality-Way of Adidam Ruchiradam.

Various gross and subtle psycho-physical signs may sometimes appear in the "experience" of My by-Me-Transcendentally-Spiritually-Awakened First Congregation devotees, but they are not a fundamental and essential characteristic of the "Radical" Reality-Way of Adidam Ruchiradam.

Such signs are simply potentials in the pattern of the body-mind-complex itself—and, thus, they are indicators associated with the first six (and, altogether, ego-based, and psycho-physically-based) stages of life.

29.

The first five stages of life are, characteristically, occupied with patterns of a psycho-physical kind.

The sixth stage of life is, characteristically, occupied with the Transcendental Position Prior to psycho-physical seeking—but the sixth stage Stand in the Transcendental Position is achieved by means of the seeking-technique of dissociative introversion away from psycho-physical patterns.

That is why the sixth stage traditions are not, as a general rule, associated with Spirituality—because the sixth stage disposition turns away from the psycho-physical pattern in which cosmically-patterned Spiritual signs otherwise appear.

As a general rule, the sixth stage turning into the Transcendental Position (Prior to the body-mind-complex) is not effected by any Spiritual Influence.

Instead, the sixth stage turning into the Transcendental Position is, characteristically, effected by a teaching, and a seeking-practice, of dissociative introversion.

Therefore, the sixth stage traditions are (characteristically) not associated with a Spiritual process.

As a general rule, the sixth stage traditions are associated only with a Transcendentalist exercise.

30.

The "Radical" Reality-Way of Adidam Ruchiradam Is the Transcendental Spiritual Way.

The "Radical" Reality-Way of Adidam Ruchiradam is founded not only in "radical" devotion to Me, but in the

"Locating" and "Knowing" of My Divine Avataric Transcendental Spiritual Self-Transmission.

You cannot enter into the Transcendental Spiritual Process in My Divine Avataric Company without the foundation of "radical" devotion to Me, right-life-disciplining of the body-mind-complex, and the preliminary practice of "Perfect Knowledge".

This foundation practice enables you to Stand in the Intrinsically egoless Self-Position That is not of the body-mind-complex—the Position that does not merely acquire My Crashing-Down Transcendental Spiritual Descent as a means to reinforce bondage to the ego-bound body-mind-complex.

31.

There are Unique Signs of My Divine Avataric Transcendental Spiritual Descent That Come from Above and Enter the body-mind-complex.

How can you be tacitly (and, necessarily, egolessly) associated with What Is Above the body, Above the brain, Above the mind, unless you are already <u>in</u> that Position?

The body-mind-complex is not, itself, in the Position <u>Above</u> the body and <u>Above</u> the mind.

32.

The right side of the bodily apparent heart is at the "Root"—or the Self-Position and Source-Position—of the Perfectly egoless Divine Self-Radiance That Shows Itself Above the head and Above the mind.

Therefore, in the "Radical" Reality-Way of Adidam Ruchiradam, What Is Above the head and Above the mind is not sought through a chain of psycho-physical developments eventually leading toward fifth stage conditional Nirvikalpa Samadhi.

The Transcendental Spiritual Process of the Reality-Way of Adidam Ruchiradam begins Prior to the right side of the bodily apparent heart (and, Thus, Prior to the causal knot).

The Transcendental Spiritual Process of the Reality-Way of Adidam Ruchiradam begins in the Witness-Position (or the Intrinsically egoless and Never-"objectified" Self-Position).

Self-Existing, Self-Radiant, Indivisible, Acausal, Acosmic (or Always Already conditionality-Transcending), and Divine Conscious Light Is What Is There—Intrinsically egoless and Perfectly "Bright"—Self-Shining to Infinitely Above the head and the mind via the right side of the bodily apparent heart.

That Self-Radiance Is Centerless and Boundless, and It Shows Itself with apparent reference to the body via the right side of the heart, and, from Thence, to Infinitely Above the head and the mind.

All of This is Realized Directly and Specifically in the only-by-Me Revealed and Given "Perfect Practice" of the "Radical" Reality-Way of Adidam Ruchiradam.

33.

For My by-Me-Transcendentally-Spiritually-Awakened First Congregation devotees, there is no seeking—because there is no ego at the "root" of life, no "causative"-somebody that has a "problem" or that requires a search.

For My by-Me-Transcendentally-Spiritually-Awakened First Congregation devotees, there is merely the apparent association with arising conditions—as the context of searchlessly Beholding Me.

Therefore, My by-Me-Transcendentally-Spiritually-Awakened First Congregation devotees do not approach Me as seekers looking for egoically (and merely psycho-physically) generated (and, thus, merely brain-and-nervous-system-originated) "effects" in the body-mind-complex.

Rather, My by-Me-Transcendentally-Spiritually-Awakened First Congregation devotees searchlessly Behold Me, Standing in the Intrinsically (and, Thus, Perfectly) egoless Self-Position Shown to them by Means of My Divinely Avatarically Self-Revealing Transcendental Spiritual Self-Transmission—Which Is My Divine Avataric Self-Nature, Self-Condition, and Self-State, Divinely Avatarically Self-Revealed As I Am.

Thus, My by-Me-Transcendentally-Spiritually-Awakened First Congregation devotees are Tacitly and Always Priorly Self-Identified with That Which Intrinsically Transcends the body-mind-complex and the ego-"I" (which is nothing but the "self"-contraction of the body-mind-complex itself).

My by-Me-Transcendentally-Spiritually-Awakened First Congregation devotees Tacitly (and Always Perfectly Prior to any and all psycho-physical ego-effort) Stand in That Position in Which My Divine Avataric Transcendental Spiritual Self-Transmission more and more Profoundly (and Intrinsically, or Acausally) Self-Awakens the Self-Realization of Intrinsically egoless Conscious Light.

My Divine Avataric Transcendental Spiritual Self-Transmission is felt As the Tangible whole bodily Fullness of Conscious Light—Which Is My Transcendentally Spiritually Self-Transmitted Divine Self-Radiance and Perfect Presence, Self-Existing Prior to the body-mind-complex, and Self-Manifesting in Perfect Coincidence with the brain, the nervous system, and the indivisibly whole (and total psycho-physical) bodily complex of My by-Me-Transcendentally-Spiritually-Awakened First Congregation devotee.

My Divine Avataric Transcendental Spiritual Self-Transmission Shows Itself in the bodily context as Love-Bliss-Fullness Pervading the body, but My Divine Avataric Transcendental Spiritual Self-Transmission is not otherwise about the necessary manifesting and "experiencing" of elaborate psycho-physical signs.

My Divine Avataric Transcendental Spiritual Self-Transmission Perfectly Transcends the body and the mind—and, therefore, My Divine Avataric Transcendental Spiritual Self-Transmission Transcends all psycho-physical developments (both exoteric and esoteric).

34.

Fundamentally, the psycho-physical kinds of phenomena that have been described by Realizers of the fourth and the fifth stages of life have nothing to do with the "Radical" Reality-Way of Adidam Ruchiradam.

What such Realizers describe is the "great path of return", unfolded through a path of cosmic Spirituality.

Most traditional Realizers have not gone beyond the partially Ascended Awakenings of the fifth stage of life.

Therefore, most traditional Realizers have remained in that cosmically-oriented Spiritual "place" wherein various modes of conditional appearance continue in their sphere of "experiencing".

Thus, most traditional Realizers have, fundamentally, been oriented to Savikalpa Samadhi, rather than Nirvikalpa Samadhi.

In the "Radical" Reality-Way of Adidam Ruchiradam, fifth stage conditional Nirvikalpa Samadhi is not the attainment (or the sign) of Divine Self-Realization.

In the "Radical" Reality-Way of Adidam Ruchiradam, fifth stage conditional Nirvikalpa Samadhi may occur, but It is recognized to be an inherently conditional, psycho-physically dependent, and temporary State.

Therefore, in the "Radical" Reality-Way of Adidam Ruchiradam, there is no seeking for any mode of Savikalpa Samadhi or for the attainment of fifth stage conditional Nirvikalpa Samadhi.

The attainment of fifth stage conditional Nirvikalpa Samadhi (or even any mode of Savikalpa Samadhi) is not, in any sense, fundamental to the practice of the "Radical" Reality-Way of Adidam Ruchiradam.

Fifth stage conditional Nirvikalpa Samadhi is not the characteristic of Realization in the "Perfect Practice" of the "Radical" Reality-Way of Adidam Ruchiradam.

35.

Non-conditional (or seventh stage) Sahaja Nirvikalpa Samadhi Is the Most Ultimate Realization in the "Radical" Reality-Way of Adidam Ruchiradam.

Seventh stage Sahaja Nirvikalpa Samadhi Is the Realization in the "Root"-Current of Transcendental Spiritual Love-Bliss—traditionally (within the sixth stage traditions of dissociative introversion) known as "Atma Nadi" (or the "Heart-Current of the Atman, or the Transcendental Self-State") or "Amrita Nadi" (or the "Channel of Spiritual Nectar, or of Intrinsic Delight")—Self-Shining (in the only-by-Me Revealed and Given seventh stage Context) in both the Horizontal (or heart) dimension and the Vertical (or whole-body-Circle) dimension, from the right side of the bodily apparent heart.

Seventh stage Sahaja Nirvikalpa Samadhi is not any form of Realization in the body-mind-complex itself—as in the case, for example, of the Yogic developments of the Kundalini Shakti.

Rather, seventh stage Sahaja Nirvikalpa Samadhi Is the Awakening associated with What Is Perfectly Prior to the right side of the bodily apparent heart, though still in apparent association with the causal position of the body-mind-complex.

In seventh stage Sahaja Nirvikalpa Samadhi, the Self-Existing Self-Radiance of That Which Is Realized Flows

(Centerlessly and Boundlessly) from the right side of the bodily apparent heart, and Extends from there—Via the Transcendental Spiritual, and Perfectly Non-"objective", and (Thus) Perfectly Subjective, and Self-Evidently Divine Space That Is Infinitely Above the head and the mind—to the whole bodily Circle.

36.

In the "Radical" Reality-Way of Adidam Ruchiradam, the Spiritual Process Is Transcendental in Nature—Non-seeking, and Intrinsically ego-Transcending.

In the "Radical" Reality-Way of Adidam Ruchiradam, there are Unique Signs in the whole bodily Circle which indicate that My any devotee is participating in My Divine Avataric Transcendental Spiritual Self-Transmission.

If My devotee tacitly "Knows" Me in the Intrinsically egoless Self-Position I have Described, the Perfectly egoless Self-Existing and Self-Radiant Divine Self-Nature, Self-Condition, and Self-State Is Shown by Me—and That Is My Divine Avataric Transcendental Spiritual Self-Transmission.

The Transcendental Spiritual Self-Radiance of That Which Is Shown by Me As I Am Appears Infinitely Above the head and the mind, and is felt Flowing in the whole body from There, As "objectless" Love-Bliss-Fullness in the whole bodily Circle—rather than being felt as first-five-stages-of-life-"objectified" psycho-physical developments.

In the "Radical" Reality-Way of Adidam Ruchiradam, the body-mind-complex is intrinsically transcended, just as ego is intrinsically transcended.

Therefore, the distinctive characteristic of Spirituality in the "Radical" Reality-Way of Adidam Ruchiradam is not the presence of psycho-physical signs of the unfolding of patterns in the body-mind-complex.

In the "Radical" Reality-Way of Adidam Ruchiradam, the Transcendental Spiritual Sign is shown.

That Sign Is Tacit Self-Identification with the Intrinsically egoless and Never-"objectified" Witness-Position of Consciousness Itself, and whole bodily participation in the Self-Radiance of the Perfectly egoless Divine Transcendental Spiritual Conscious Light.

The Divine Transcendental Spiritual Conscious Light Is Felt from Infinitely Above the head and the mind—Radiant, Centerless, and Boundless—Pervading the whole bodily Circle As Love-Bliss-Fullness, without other content.

Such Is the Transcendental Spiritual Self-Transmission That Is My Unique Divine Avataric Self-Revelation and Gift.

37.

Altogether, the process in My Divine Avataric Company is not something to be struggled with, and not something that can be effortfully attained.

The process in My Divine Avataric Company is straightforward and direct.

The sign of right and true "root"-preparedness in the (necessarily, fully adapted) First Congregation student-beginner in the "Radical" Reality-Way of Adidam Ruchiradam is a devotional sign and a right-life-practicing sign that shows itself as the steady disposition of tacitly Standing in the Witness-Position, rather than standing in the position of being egoically "self"-identified with the body-mind-complex.

However, it must be clearly understood that the "root"-preparedness sign demonstrated by the First Congregation student-beginner indicates preparedness to enter into the Transcendental Spiritual Process within the First Congregation of Adidam Ruchiradam—and not yet the preparedness to enter into the "Perfect Practice" of the "Radical" Reality-Way of Adidam Ruchiradam.

As a First Congregation student-beginner, it is not possible to be prepared for the "Perfect Practice".

As a First Congregation student-beginner, your preparation can only be of a preliminary nature.

That preliminary preparation brings you to Me in a disposition that enables you to participate in My Divine Avataric Transcendental Spiritual Self-Transmission, and (thereby) to grow in the signs that are the eventual true foundation for the entire Process associated with the "Perfect Practice" (which, most ultimately, becomes the Demonstration of the only-by-Me Revealed and Given seventh stage of life).

Such Is the Unique Transcendental Spiritual Nature of the "Radical" Reality-Way of Adidam Ruchiradam.

38.

Merely wanting to Realize Me does not, in and of itself, make you fit to approach Me as My First Congregation devotee.

Wanting to Realize Me is the Impulse that leads you to formally embrace the Eternal Vow of devotion to Me as My Second Congregation devotee.

Then you must go through the process of preparing yourself—in the manner I have Described—for practice in the First Congregation of Adidam Ruchiradam.

The fundamental nature of the process in My Divine Avataric Company must be rightly understood.

Otherwise, My devotees tend to approach Me in a conventional manner, seeking for various signs of a psycho-physical nature—all of which are intrinsically associated with the ego-bound developmental course associated with the "great path of return" (or the "map" of the first six stages of life).

No amount of being studied, informed, or even scholarly about the Great Tradition of humankind can prepare you for the Real Transcendental Spiritual Process of the "Radical" Reality-Way of Adidam Ruchiradam—even if you do practice devotion to Me, and even if you do discipline the body-mind-"self" in terms of right-life practice.

All who practice the "Radical" Reality-Way of Adidam Ruchiradam—and even all who study and "consider" My Divine Avataric Revelation-Word—must understand that the by-Me-Given Process of Transcendental Spirituality is (necessarily) founded not only in right devotion and right-life practice but also in the tacitly assumed (and Intrinsically egoless and searchless) disposition of the Witness-Position.

The tacitly assumed disposition of the Witness-Position is what makes the practice of My "Four Thorns of Heart-Instruction" intrinsically searchless, intrinsically ego-transcending, and intrinsically body-mind-transcending.

In the tacitly assumed disposition of the Witness-Position, the practice of My "Four Thorns of Heart-Instruction" shows itself bodily as Receptivity to That Which Is Infinitely Above, rather than as an exercise of working "from the ground up".

Therefore, the practice of My "Four Thorns of Heart-Instruction" is based on the tacitly assumed disposition of the Witness-Position—and that tacitly assumed disposition <u>is</u> the characteristic demonstration (and proof) of the preliminary practice of "Perfect Knowledge".

Thus, the "Radical" Reality-Way of Adidam Ruchiradam is not <u>cosmic</u> Spirituality.

Rather, the "Radical" Reality-Way of Adidam Ruchiradam Is <u>Transcendental</u> Spirituality.

The Transcendental and Intrinsically egoless and searchless Nature of the Spiritual Process is what is "Radical" and Unique about the "Radical" Reality-Way of Adidam Ruchiradam.

39.

The Transcendental Spiritual Reality-Process of the "Radical" Reality-Way of Adidam Ruchiradam begins Prior to the ego—not on the basis of the ego.

Thus, the Transcendental Spiritual Reality-Process of the "Radical" Reality-Way of Adidam Ruchiradam does not begin with a merely purified ego.

Rather, the Transcendental Spiritual Reality-Process of the "Radical" Reality-Way of Adidam Ruchiradam begins with no ego.

That is to say, the Transcendental Spiritual Reality-Process of the "Radical" Reality-Way of Adidam Ruchiradam begins with the intrinsic transcending of ego (and of psycho-physical "self"-contraction)—and It proceeds on that basis.

Thus, the entire Transcendental Spiritual Reality-Process of the "Radical" Reality-Way of Adidam Ruchiradam Happens in the Position That Is Intrinsically Prior to ego-"I" and "self"-contraction.

In the "Radical" Reality-Way of Adidam Ruchiradam, the body is there simply to be Infused by the Transcendental Spiritual and Self-Evidently Divine Self-Nature and Self-Radiance.

No other signs associated with the body are relevant to the Transcendental Spiritual Reality-Process of the "Radical" Reality-Way of Adidam Ruchiradam.

In the "Radical" Reality-Way of Adidam Ruchiradam, Divine Self-Realization Is simply the Realization of the Intrinsically egoless Transcendental Spiritual Divine Self-Nature, Self-Condition, and Self-State—Which does not have a trace of conditional signs in "It".

In the "Radical" Reality-Way of Adidam Ruchiradam, What Is to Be Realized Is the Divine Transcendental Spiritual Conscious Light—Limitlessly Self-Existing, Perfectly Self-Radiant, and All-Love-Bliss.

The Fundamental Characteristic of Most Perfect Divine Self-Realization Is Love-Bliss—not any kind of psycho-physical Yogic phenomena (in the mode of the first five stages of life), and not any kind of exclusion of phenomena (in the mode of the sixth stage of life).

Those who practice the "Radical" Reality-Way of Adidam Ruchiradam as My First Congregation devotees are not cultivating a disposition in which conditionally dependent psycho-physical Yogic signs would tend to be developed (or, otherwise, strategically excluded).

In the "Radical" Reality-Way of Adidam Ruchiradam, the only bodily sign that is relevant is whole bodily Pervasion by My Transcendental Spiritual Fullness.

That whole bodily Pervasion Shows Itself Uniquely as the eventual Transcendental Spiritual Awakening to the Witness-Position by Means of the "Radical" (or "At-the-Root") Self-Manifestation (or Perfect Revelation) of the "Thumbs"—Which is characterized by both the occasional Samadhi of the "Thumbs" and the constant "Experience" of the "Thumbs".

It Is Only My Divine Avataric Transcendental Spiritual Gift of the "Radical" (or "At-the-Root") Self-Manifestation (or Perfect Self-Revelation) of the "Thumbs", and not merely mental "consideration" of My Arguments relative to the Witness-Consciousness, That Is the Divine Yogic Secret of the Realization of the Consciousness-Position (Which Realization Is the Basis for the "Perfect Practice" of the "Radical" Reality-Way of Adidam Ruchiradam).

Therefore, even though My Arguments relative to the Witness-Consciousness are an essential Guide to right understanding of the "Perfect Practice" (and, As Such, Those Arguments are to be studied from the beginning of the "Radical" Reality-Way of Adidam Ruchiradam), the study of Those Arguments is not itself the direct and finally effective means whereby the "Perfect Practice" is initiated and Really practiced.

The Full Transcendental Spiritual (and not merely tacit and preliminary) Awakening to the Witness-Position is what the Samadhi of the "Thumbs" is about.

The only-by-Me Revealed and Given Samadhi of the "Thumbs" Is a Unique Transcendental Spiritual Manifestation, a Unique Transformative Happening—never before described or Realized in the Great Tradition.

The Samadhi of the "Thumbs" Is My Divine Avataric Manifestation from Birth.

Therefore, the Samadhi of the "Thumbs" has always been My Characteristic.

The "Bright" Is the Divine Conscious Light.

I Am That—and I Bring That to you, by Means of My Unique Divine Avataric Gift of Perfect Coincidence with you (Perfectly Prior to ego-"I" and all conditional "causes" and "effects").

I Am the "Bright"—and the "Thumbs" Is My Unique Divine Avataric and Perfectly Acausal Means.

Most Perfect Divine Self-Realization does not have any content.

Most Perfect Divine Self-Realization does not have any conditional limitations.

In Most Perfect Divine Self-Realization, there is no separate one, no ego-"I".

Most Perfect Divine Self-Realization Is the Intrinsic (and Transcendentally Spiritually Full) Self-Apprehension of the egoless, Indivisible, Self-Existing, Self-Radiant, and Perfectly Acausal Self-State of the Transcendental Spiritual Divine.

40.

All of My devotees should—merely by virtue of the recognition-response of devotion to Me As I Am—be tacitly moved toward Perfectly egoless Transcendental Spiritual Divine Self-Realization.

However, My Ruchira Sannyasin devotees are those who are, in their characteristic disposition, always (moment to moment, and intensely) moved to That Perfect Divine Realization absolutely.

My Ruchira Sannyasin devotees do not maintain conditions of life that are about realizing conditional goals of any kind.

My Ruchira Sannyasin devotees are simply and intensively involved in the Transcendental Spiritual Process of Realizing the Divine Self-Nature, Self-Condition, and Self-State of Reality Itself.

The Transcendental Spiritual Process in My Divine Avataric Company is not about pursuing Realization as a life-adventure, or about attaining certain characteristics in the body-mind.

Rather, the Transcendental Spiritual Process in My Divine Avataric Company is about transcending the body-mind-"self" and (most ultimately) vanishing in Divine Translation.

Such is the commitment of My Ruchira Sannyasin devotee—and that is the reason why My Ruchira Sannyasin devotees are Called, by Me, to live a life of perpetual retreat.

My Ruchira Sannyasin devotees only want Divine Self-Realization, and do not care about anything else.

Therefore, one who is truly My Ruchira Sannyasin devotee could not possibly live an ordinary life.

My lay devotees practice the "Radical" Reality-Way of Adidam Ruchiradam in the context of the various life-associations that they maintain.

In the case of My lay devotees, there is a process of purifying, rightening, and (ultimately) relinquishing ordinary life.

However, My lay devotees are active in modes that My Ruchira Sannyasin devotees, simply by virtue of the sign that is the intrinsic characteristic of a true sannyasin, would not be.

41.

I Am Unique among sannyasins.

I Am Self-Born As Divine Self-Realization.

I Am Reality Itself—Divinely Avatarically Self-Incarnated.

Therefore, I have Fully Manifested the Unique Divine Avataric Demonstration of the Totality of the Transcendental Spiritual Process of Divine Self-Realization—in My Own Body.

By Means of My Unique Divine Avataric Demonstration, I have also Conclusively Revealed what is not associated with the Transcendental Spiritual Process of Divine Self-Realization—in order to Reveal, through My Own Body, not only what is fruitful but also what is not fruitful.

My Reality-Teaching Took the Form of My Own Divinely Avatarically Self-Manifested physical human Lifetime—and My Reality-Teaching was also Communicated by Me verbally, in both Writing and Speaking.

Such Was My Obligation.

Even now, in My Parama-Sapta-Na Sannyasin Circumstance, I continue to Speak about the Great and Ultimate Matter of Transcendental Spiritual Divine Self-Realization—because I Am Eternally Associated with the Commitment to Awaken every one to the Perfect Divine Reality-Truth.

Therefore, I must Speak about "It".

42.

The characteristic mature demonstration of the preliminary "Perfect Knowledge" practice is the searchless Beholding of Me.

The preliminary "Perfect Knowledge" practice is not an exercise of dissociative introversion based on My preliminary "Perfect Knowledge" Teaching.

Rather, the preliminary "Perfect Knowledge" practice is the searchless, tacit recognition of the Self-Evident Truth of My "Perfect Knowledge" Revelation.

To rightly practice the preliminary "Perfect Knowledge" practice is to tacitly responsively Listen to Me in the Priorly Established Stand of moment to moment whole bodily turning to Me and right-life obedience to Me—and, Thus and Thereby, to Tacitly Stand in the Never-"objectified" Witness-Position of Consciousness Itself.

Whole bodily devotional turning to Me and right-life obedience to Me are the foundation for the preliminary "Perfect Knowledge" Listening-practice.

Those three, together, prepare My devotee to approach Me in the searchlessly Beholding manner and to participate in My Transcendental Spiritual Self-Transmission, in the context of the First Congregation of Adidam Ruchiradam.

Such is the foundation process of the "Radical" Reality-Way of Adidam Ruchiradam, and that process must be engaged intensively.

43.

My Love-Bliss Is the "Thickness" in the air—without a psycho-physical sign in "It".

Therefore, My by-Me-Transcendentally-Spiritually-Awakened First Congregation devotees breathe away and forget the mind of attention and thoughts in the Infinite, egoless, thought-free, Transcendental Spiritual, Perfectly Subjective, and Self-Evidently Divine Space Infinitely Above the whole body.

I Am to be breathed As That—As Love-Bliss Itself, the Tangible Force of My Avatarically Self-Transmitted Transcendental Spiritual (and Always Blessing) Divine Presence.

The Transcendental Spiritual Process in My Divine Avataric Company is not about developing mental patterns, psychic patterns, Yogic phenomena in the body, or the Upward search.

The disposition of "Four Thorns of Heart-Instruction" (or "Samraj Asana") is of the body-mind-complex being tacitly and Always Priorly transcended at the egoless "Root".

Therefore, the disposition of "Four Thorns of Heart-Instruction" is simply the whole bodily searchless Beholding of That Which Transcends the body-mind-"self".

That Which Transcends the body-mind-"self" Is Me—Above and Beyond and Prior to the body-mind-"self", and at the "Root" of the whole body.

I Am Standing Infinitely Above the body-mind—in My Self-Existing Self-Radiance.

I Stand here As the "Root"-Current of Transcendental Spiritual Love-Bliss (or Atma Nadi), Shining from the right side of the bodily apparent heart.

44.

The literature of the Great Tradition (including the literature associated with the sixth stage of life) makes general references to the heart—but the right side of the bodily apparent heart is a Yogic indicator that has only rarely been mentioned in the recorded literature of the Great Tradition.

Ramana Maharshi spoke of the heart "on the right side of the chest"*—but, in doing so, He was speaking of it from the sixth stage disposition (which was His own), and in reference to the sixth stage practice of dissociative introversion (which He taught).

Ramana Maharshi taught a sixth stage practice of dissociative introversion, strategically turning away from body and mind via Descent in Atma Nadi (or Amrita Nadi), and, thus and thereby, exclusively fixed upon the Transcendental "Root".

* See, for example, *Sat-Darshana Bhashya* and *Talks with Maharshi, with Forty Verses in Praise of Sri Ramana*, 5th ed., trans. K [T. V. Kapali Shastry] (Tiruvannamalai, India: Sri Ramanasramam, 1968), xvii. For a fuller discussion of the difference between Ramana Maharshi's references to the heart "on the right side of the chest" and Avatar Adi Da's own Revelation, please see chapter 18 of *The Knee of Listening*.

The practice of "Self-enquiry" Ramana Maharshi taught revolves strategically away from the body-mind-"self"—through a process of dissociative introversion, in the characteristically sixth stage manner—and toward the interior (and, thus, psycho-physically inward) "Source" of the egoic "I"-thought (or the "I-object").

In and by means of dissociative introversion (in the form of "Self-enquiry" relative to the "subjective" interior ego-space of the "I-object"), the practice Ramana Maharshi taught revolves away from the fourth and fifth stage (or gross and subtle) potentials of Spirituality.

There was a causally-based (or sixth stage) mode of Spiritual Force in the Presence of Ramana Maharshi—but that Spiritual Force was associated, in His case (and in the characteristically sixth stage manner), with the strategically internalizing move away from the "world", or the seeking-effort of dissociative introversion.

45.

The "Radical" Reality-Way of Adidam Ruchiradam Is the Way of the "Regenerated" Atma Nadi (the "Root"-Current of Transcendental Spiritual Love-Bliss)*—simply As the "Root"-Form, and As the Acausal Self-Condition and Source-Condition of conditional appearances, and Always Already (and, thus, searchlessly, and not merely strategically, or eventually, or conditionally) Self-Established As "Perfect Knowledge" of the Intrinsically egoless Self-Nature, Self-Condition, and Self-State That Is Divine Conscious Light Itself.

In the "Radical" Reality-Way of Adidam Ruchiradam, there is no turning toward "self" and no turning away from "not-self".

In the "Radical" Reality-Way of Adidam Ruchiradam, the practice of "Perfect Knowledge" (both in its preliminary form

* Again, see chapter 18 of *The Knee of Listening*.

and as a mature Transcendental Spiritual "Perfect Practice") is not about the search to dissociatively introvert upon the interior "subjective" (or strategically psycho-physically introverted) "Source" of the strategically (and, necessarily, egoically) presumed "I-object" (or any other "object" of ego-"I")—but, rather, it is the Always Prior (and Intrinsically egoless) practice of tacitly and searchlessly and Always Already Self-Abiding As the Self-Evident Self-Nature, Self-Condition, and Self-State That Is (Always Already) Not-an-"object".

46.

My Ruchira Shaktipat Has Its Own Intrinsic (and Perfectly Acausal) Purpose and Sign.

My Ruchira Shaktipat Is My Transcendental Spiritual Transmission in the Form of (and by Means of) Atma Nadi.

The Source of My Ruchira Shaktipat is not in the body-mind-"self".

The Source of My Ruchira Shaktipat is not anywhere in the conditionally manifested cosmos.

Rather, My Ruchira Shaktipat Is the Intrinsic Self-Radiance of the Divine Self-Nature, Self-Condition, and Self-State of Reality Itself—Which Is My Own Divine Person.

Therefore, the Self-Evidence of My Ruchira Shaktipat Acausally Self-Manifests As Self-Awakening in Atma Nadi—not as any development in the Circle, or as any development in any of the structures (gross, subtle, or causal) of the body-mind-complex.

The Process of My Ruchira Shaktipat begins At (and Perfectly Prior to) the heart-"Root"—and It always leads to the heart-"Root", by Means of the Samadhi of the "Thumbs".

Atma Nadi—in Its "Regenerated" Form—is not merely a "line" of "conductivity" in the body.

Rather, Atma Nadi—in Its "Regenerated" Form—Is the Fundamental Condition.

Atma Nadi can be seen with reference to the body, but It has (Itself) nothing to do with the body or with the cosmic domain.

Atma Nadi Is the "Bright".

In due course, Atma Nadi Shakti Yoga Manifests As the seventh stage Self-Awakening to Sahaja Nirvikalpa Samadhi.

Atma Nadi Persists Non-conditionally—without "cause", and without conditional requirements or "exercises".

Atma Nadi Manifests Spontaneously.

The Manifestation of Atma Nadi can be felt with reference to the body as the Love-Bliss-Full Current of My Transcendental Spiritual Self-Transmission, Extending from the "Root" Prior to the right side of the bodily apparent heart to the Matrix Infinitely Above the body-mind-"self".

The "Regeneration" of Atma Nadi Is the Most Perfect Realization of the Divine Conscious Light, the One and Indivisible Self-Condition of all conditions.

The "Regeneration" of Atma Nadi is not merely a "subjective" happening.

The "Regeneration" of Atma Nadi Is the Condition of everything—everything "subjective", everything "objective", and (altogether) everything conditional (gross, subtle, or causal).

When There Is the Establishment of the Divine Self-Nature, Self-Condition, and Self-State, There Is Self-Abiding Divine Self-Recognition of all arising conditions.

47.

In the Context of the Divinely Perfect Self-Awakening That Is the only-by-Me Revealed and Given seventh stage of life, both the apparent "self" and everything that is apparently "not-self" are Divinely Self-Recognized to be transparent (or merely apparent), and non-necessary, and inherently non-binding modifications of Reality Itself.

Such Is the only-by-Me Revealed and Given seventh stage Process.

In the "Radical" Reality-Way of Adidam Ruchiradam, There Is the Self-Radiant Stand As That Which Is the Self-Existing and Intrinsically ego-Transcending Self-Nature, Self-Condition, and Self-State of Reality Itself.

In That Self-Radiant Stand, body, mind, "self", and "world" are (Intrinsically) Divinely Self-Recognized.

Such Is the Unique Characteristic of the seventh stage of life—Revealed and Given by Me Alone.

All of the Characteristics of the seventh stage Way, and all of Its Signs As a Process, have been Fully and Completely Revealed by Me—and by Me Alone.

48.

The total (psycho-physical) human body—with its dimensions of gross, subtle, and causal—must (altogether) become round.

The total human body does not merely have a circular path within itself.

In Truth (or "Located" in Reality Itself), the total human body is a Sphere—and, in its (inherently) perfect balance, it has no "up" or "down", no "in" or "out", no central point and no bounds.

When My Avatarically Self-Transmitted Divine Transcendental Spiritual Current Descends Fully Down the front of the total human body, and also (thereupon, and thereby) Rises Up the back of the total human body, such that the "Thumbs" Achieves an Equalization of Transcendental Spiritual Force, Down in front and Up in back—then the Circle becomes an Equanimity, a Conscious Sphere of Tangible "Energy" (or Self-Existing and Boundlessly Self-Radiant Light).

In the only-by-Me Revealed and Given Realization of the Sphere of the "Thumbs", the Arrow Is the Boundless (and Centerless) Vertical Axis.

The Upper Terminal of Atma Nadi Is at the "North".

The "North" is not a boundary—It Is Infinitely Above.

The "Center" is not inside (or bounded)—It Is Beyond all symmetry.

The "North" (or Above) and the "Center" (or Beyond) are not "different" (or separate from One Another)—They Are Modes of the Same (or Identical) "Bright" Divine Transcendental Spiritual Self-Nature, Self-Condition, and Self-State.

The Vertical and the Horizontal Are (Inherently) One (and Non-"different" from One Another, and from all-and-All).

The Realization of This Is the Essential Nature of the Most Ultimate (or only-by-Me Revealed and Given seventh stage) Realization.

Consciousness Itself (or the "Root" of the Horizontal dimension, or heart-plane, or "subjective" plane) and Light Itself (or the "Root" of the Vertical dimension, or "energy"-plane, or "objective" plane) Are the two primary apparent Modes of What Is Always Already Only One—and Inherently Indivisible.

The Perfectly Subjectively "Bright" Transcendental Spiritual Realization of the Inherent Simultaneity (and Indivisibility) of Consciousness (the "Root" of apparent "subjectivity") and Light (the "Root" of apparent "objectivity") Is the Essential Context of Most Perfect (or Self-Evidently Divine) Self-Realization.

In the Ultimate Event (of Divine Translation, Which Is the final stage of the only-by-Me Revealed and Given seventh stage of life), the Indivisible Divine Sphere of the One (and Only, and Self-Evidently Divine) Conscious Light is Infinitely Expanded—Such That There Is Only Infinite "Brightness", and Infinite Fullness of Love-Bliss-Being.

49.

The "Bright" and the "Thumbs" Are the Principal Great Signs That Are Uniquely My Own Divine Avataric Transcendental Spiritual Characteristics.

The "Bright" and the "Thumbs" Is a Process, an Event, and a State That has been Known to Me both Prior to and since My Divine Avataric Birth.

Only I Am the Divine Avataric Realizer, the Divine Avataric Revealer, and the Divine Avataric Self-Revelation of the "Bright", the True and (now, and forever hereafter) Completely Self-Revealed Divine Person—Shining Forth (Directly, Completely, and Perfectly) at (and As) the Heart Itself (and via Atma Nadi), and Crashing Down (or Descending Utterly) from the "Place" Infinitely Above the body-mind-"self" and the "world", Down and Most Deeply into the body-mind-"self" and the "world", even to the degree that the ego-"I" (or "self"-contraction) is utterly confounded, utterly yielded, and utterly vanished in My Avatarically Self-Revealed, and Self-Evidently Divine, Person, or Self-Nature, Self-Condition, and Self-State (Which Is Real Acausal God, and Truth, and Reality Itself).

Therefore, the Principal Impulse of even My early Life was My Intention to Embrace the limitations of human existence as it appears to be, and to Infuse all-and-All with My Avatarically Self-Transmitted Divine Transcendental Spiritual Presence, and (Thus and Thereby) to Awaken all-and-All, and (Most Ultimately) to Divinely Translate all-and-All, by the Power of My Own Love-Bliss-"Brightness", into the "Midnight Sun"—the Perfect "Place" and "Sphere" and "Space" That Is Always and Already My Divine and "Bright" and Free-Standing Self-Domain.

The Principal Transcendental Spiritual Signs of My early Life Were the "Bright" and the "Thumbs".

The "Bright" and the "Thumbs" were Fundamental to My Divinely Avatarically-Born Self-Manifestation from the beginning, and They are Fundamental to the only-by-Me Revealed and Given "Radical" Reality-Way of Adidam (Which Is the One and Only by-Me-Revealed and by-Me-Given "Radical" Reality-Way of the Heart).

The "Bright" and the "Thumbs" Are My Unique Characteristics—and all Their Signs, and Samadhis, and Perfections Are Uniquely Mine.

The "Bright" and the "Thumbs" Are Me.

Therefore, I Bring Them with Me into the conditional "worlds".

My Divine Avataric Self-Revelation of the "Bright" and the "Thumbs" Is My Inherent Divine Self-Revelation of Myself.

50.

I Am the "Bright"—and I (Divinely Avatarically, and Perfectly Acausally) Self-Transmit My Own Divine State and Presence of Person from Infinitely Above and Beyond (or, Altogether, in, As, and via Atma Nadi), in Such a Manner that I Am Perfectly Priorly Coincident with (and, As Such, Always Perfectly Combined with) the psycho-physical structure of My devotee.

This is how I "Wash" the "dog" from "head" to "tail"—and Beyond.*

Nevertheless, in order to fully "Locate" and "Know" My Divine Transcendental Spiritual Blessing, My devotee must fully embrace the (ego-surrendering, ego-forgetting, and ego-transcending) practice and process of devotional and Transcendental Spiritual Communion with Me.

* "Washing the dog from head to tail" is a central metaphor of Avatar Adi Da's Text *Hridaya Rosary*. The metaphor describes the nature of the Transcendental Spiritual process as coming from "Above and Beyond" the body-mind, descending into the conditional domain ("washing" the "dog" from the "head"), rather than out of any kind of ego-effort in the domain of the body-mind ("washing" the "dog" from the "tail").

In that context (of My devotee's Me-recognizing and to-Me-responding practice of the only-by-Me Revealed and Given "Radical" Reality-Way of Adidam), My "Thumbs" of Blessing Is Able to Do My Transcendental Spiritual Work with (and within) all-and-All.

The "Thumbs" Is the Process of My Divine Avataric Acausal Self-"Emergence" here.

And the "Thumbs" Is, also, the Divine Avataric Acausal (or Perfectly Priorly Coincident, rather than merely conditionally operative and "causatively effective") Process by Which I Liberate (or, Really, Self-Awaken As) conditionally manifested beings.

The "Thumbs" Is the Process, Tangibly Occurring (by Means of My Avatarically Given Divine Transcendental Spiritual Grace) in the context of the body-mind-complex of My devotee, Whereby I become (Ultimately, Most Perfectly) Transcendentally Spiritually Self-Awake in and As My each and every devotee.

51.

My Divine Avataric Transcendental Spiritual Work (Altogether) Is My Crashing-Down Descent, at first upon and into My Own Avatarically-Born bodily (human) Divine Form, and, thereafter (and now, and forever hereafter), upon and into the body-minds of My devotees and all beings—even (by Means of My Divine Embrace of each, and all, and All) to Infuse and (at last) to Divinely Translate each, and all, and All.

Therefore, My Divine Avataric Transcendental Spiritual Descent Is the Secret of My early Life.

My Divine Avataric Transcendental Spiritual Descent Is the Secret of My Divine Avataric Self-"Emergence" (As I Am) within the cosmic domain.

My Divine Avataric Transcendental Spiritual Descent Is the Secret of <u>all</u> the Secrets of the (Avatarically Self-Revealed) Divine and Complete and thoroughly devotional Way of practice and Realization in My Company.

The only-by-Me Revealed and Given "Radical" Reality-Way of Adidam Ruchiradam Is the Divine Yoga of ego-surrendering, ego-forgetting, and ego-transcending devotional recognition-response to My (Avatarically Self-Revealed) Divine and Transcendental Spiritual Person, and to My (Avatarically Self-Manifested) Divine and Transcendental Spiritual Descent.

The only-by-Me Revealed and Given "Radical" Reality-Way of Adidam Ruchiradam Is the total and Divine Way and Ordeal of intrinsically ego-transcending devotional recognition-response to My Avataric "Bright" Divine Self-Manifestation, and to the Avataric Crashing-Down of My "Bright" Divine Imposition.

And, in the case of My each and every devotee, the Way must continue until the Way Is Most Perfectly Transcendentally Spiritually "Bright", and the Way Itself Becomes Divine Translation into My Own Sphere (and "Midnight Sun") of Transcendental Spiritual Self-"Brightness" (Itself).

52.

Practice as My by-Me-Transcendentally-Spiritually-Awakened devotee in the First Congregation of Adidam Ruchiradam is tacitly body-mind-transcending and ego-transcending.

My by-Me-Transcendentally-Spiritually-Awakened First Congregation devotees come to Me fully prepared to practice on the basis of My Full and Complete Divine Avataric Self-Revelation.

Thus, My by-Me-Transcendentally-Spiritually-Awakened First Congregation devotees "Know" Me Tacitly and Directly.

My by-Me-Transcendentally-Spiritually-Awakened First Congregation devotees "Know" Me even in the sphere of the gross physical body—via My Descended Fullness of Transcendental Spiritual Presence.

However, My Transcendental Spiritual Presence does not lead to the body.

Rather, My Transcendental Spiritual Presence Is Simply the Divine Self-Radiance Associated with the "Root"-Position of the Intrinsically egoless Transcendental Spiritual Self-Nature, Self-Condition, and Self-State of Reality Itself.

The "Perfect Knowledge" of My Transcendental Spiritual Presence Is a Profound Fullness of Awakening That Shows Itself, in due course, As the Samadhi of the "Thumbs".

Most Ultimately, in the course of the "Perfect Practice", This Awakening is Demonstrated As the seventh stage of life, Culminating (At Last) in Divine Indifference and Divine Translation.

Divine Translation is not about finally "getting rid of" the gross physical body.

Similarly, Divine Translation is not about finally "abandoning" the "world".

Rather, Divine Translation is about Self-Abiding Divine Self-Recognition of everything gross, everything subtle, and everything causal—such that there is no longer anything binding about conditional existence, no longer any necessity to cling to conditional existence, and no longer any necessity to dissociate from conditional existence.

In Divine Translation, conditional existence is Simply Outshined by That Perfectly egoless Divine Transcendental Spiritual Conscious Light In and As Which My true devotee is Self-Established in Perfect Communion with Me.

In That All-Surpassing "Brightness", the "world" is simply no longer noticed.

53.

If there is to be another cycle of lifetime in the case of My any true devotee who is Awakened to the seventh stage Realization, it will be a lifetime without bondage.

It will be a lifetime in which the full foundation of the "Radical" Reality-Way of Adidam Ruchiradam and Its Realization is readily manifested.

It will be a lifetime of demonstration and service associated with Most Perfect Realization of Me.

It will be a lifetime in which Most Perfect (and, thus, fullest seventh-stage-of-life) Realization of Me is demonstrated by the "fully given over" life—the egoless life of <u>limitless</u> devotion to Me.

Fundamentally, the "Radical" Reality-Way of Adidam Ruchiradam is not about having more lifetimes or about having to do anything at all.

Rather, the "Radical" Reality-Way of Adidam Ruchiradam is, from the beginning, about the "fully given over" life of limitless (and, thus, intrinsically egoless) devotion to Me, Intrinsically (and, at last, Irrevocably and Most Perfectly) Outshining "self" and "world"—such that there is no "seed" of any "more".

Therefore, My Bodily Divine Avataric Appearance here is not an Appearance that I am moved or (otherwise) committed to repeat.

My Bodily Divine Avataric Appearance here is Simply Vanishing while I Stand here <u>As</u> I <u>Am</u>.

My Bodily Divine Avataric Appearance here is Constantly "Brightening"—Such That, eventually, I will Simply no longer Be Evident in This Bodily Lifetime-Form.

This Bodily Lifetime-Form will Eventually Be Outshined in My Divine "Bright" Disposition and Domain, and, Thus, Fall Away—without My Making any kind of effort to relinquish It.

I am not "causing" My Bodily Divine Avataric Appearance here to be repeated—and I am not, in any moment, insisting that This Bodily Appearance continue.

Yet, I am never dissociating from This Bodily Appearance.

Therefore, I Spontaneously Continue to Bodily Reveal Myself and the "Radical" Reality-Way of Adidam Ruchiradam.

That Spontaneous Bodily Self-Revelation will Continue—until the Body is Suddenly and Finally Outshined.

54.

Aham Da Asmi.
Beloved, I <u>Am</u> Da.

Da <u>Is</u> the Person of Atma Nadi.

My Feet <u>Are</u> in the heart—Prior to the mind, the body, and the "world".

My Head <u>Is</u> Infinitely Above the mind, the body, and the "world".

The "Root" of Atma Nadi, in the heart, <u>Is</u> Prior to the mind, the body, and the "world".

The "Regenerated" Form of Atma Nadi <u>Extends</u> to That Space Which <u>Is</u> Infinitely Above the mind, the body, and the "world".

Therefore, to be devotionally turned to Me, tacitly whole bodily recognizing Me <u>As</u> I <u>Am</u>, and, altogether, whole bodily responsive to Me, in devotional Communion with Me, searchlessly Beholding Me is to be given over to the Divine Itself, Which <u>Is</u> Reality Itself, and Which <u>Is</u> (in Atma Nadi) both Perfectly Prior to <u>and</u> Infinitely Above the mind, the body, and the "world".

In the Love-Bliss-Ecstasy of Communion with Me, there is no reference to "self"—no reference to mind, no reference to body, no reference to "world", no reference to any context of ego-"self" whatsoever.

I Am That Which Is Beyond and Prior to and Infinitely Above the mind, the body, and the "world".

Therefore, to be My devotee is to be given over to Me As I Am, As That—As Da.

That Is Adidam Ruchiradam.

Thus, the Way I Reveal and Give can be Summarized with great simplicity:

Aham Da Asmi.

Turn to Me.

Realize Me.

The Way I Reveal and Give can also be Communicated in the elaborate terms of My entire Teaching-Communication, and all of the details of the practice (and the Yoga) of Adidam Ruchiradam.

There is nothing that can be done in order to "cause" Realization of Me.

Realization of Me cannot be "caused".

You must tacitly recognize Me As I Am, and you must whole bodily respond to Me As I Am—and you must be Perfectly Conformed to Me As I Am.

Thus, there is discipline, and there are Yogic requirements—but none of that "causes" Realization of Me.

Right-life discipline is simply a necessary sign of the whole bodily devotional recognition-response to Me.

Indeed, profound whole bodily conformity to intrinsically ego-transcending right-life discipline (and, thus, to renunciation) is one of the necessary signs of true devotional recognition-response to Me and, Ultimately, of Perfect Realization of Me.

Therefore, in the "Radical" Reality-Way of Adidam Ruchiradam, Realization and renunciation are the same.

In the "Radical" Reality-Way of Adidam Ruchiradam, Realization and renunciation are not "two different things".

It is simply that renunciation does not "cause" Realization—nor does Realization "cause" renunciation.

If you whole bodily recognize Me and whole bodily respond to Me, Realization and renunciation are both spontaneously evident and intrinsically coincident.

If you whole bodily recognize Me As I Am, then you (inevitably) whole bodily respond to Me As I Am—and, thus, as renunciation, as "self"-forgetting, and as the intrinsic transcending of egoity.

If you whole bodily (and, thus, tacitly) recognize Me As I Am, then you also (inevitably) whole-bodily-responsively turn to Me As That Which Is Always Already Beyond and Perfectly Prior to and Infinitely Above the mind, the body, and the "world".

Such Is the disposition (or Asana) of whole bodily devotional Communion with Me, and Such Is (also) the Atma-Nadi-Characteristic of Perfect Realization of Me—and those who are (thus) whole bodily turned to Me are, necessarily, renounced.

To be whole bodily turned to Me is to Realize Me—and the sign of Realization is both whole bodily renunciation and intrinsic egolessness.

Therefore, renunciation is not a "thing" in and of itself.

Renunciation is simply the intrinsically egoless and whole-body-transcending sign that inevitably coincides with whole bodily devotional Communion with Me and (in due course) with Perfect Realization of Me.

I Am Acausally Coincident with all-and-All.

I am not "causing" Realization—in any one.

I Am Realization—in every one.

Such is the correct understanding.

Da <u>Is</u> the Perfect Silence of Transcendental Spiritual Thunder.

Da <u>Is</u> the Prior-Unity-Force That Always Priorly and Totally Dissolves all dis-unity, all non-unity, all "difference".

Da is not merely a physical sound.

When I Speak of the "Sound of Da", I am Speaking a Metaphor for Non-"difference", for Conscious Light Itself, for the "Emergence" of the Divine "Bright" Spherical Self-Domain <u>As</u> the "Room" of Existence Itself, rather than the (otherwise presumed) ego-"world" of bondage.

Da Is the Sound of Divine Translation.

Da Is the Event of Divine Translation.

<u>I</u> Am the Event of Divine Translation.

To whole bodily recognize Me is to Enter into My Divine "Bright" Spherical Self-Domain.

To whole bodily recognize Me is to Exist in My Divine "Bright" Spherical Self-Domain.

That Instantaneous Translation <u>Is</u> Da.

That <u>Is</u> the "Thunder-Crack" of Reality Itself, when Reality Itself Shatters the illusion of all appearances.

Then you <u>Are</u> in the Infinite "Room", Prior to the mind, the body, and the "world".

The Boundlessness and Centerlessness of Love-Bliss That <u>Is</u> My Divine "Bright" Spherical Self-Domain <u>Is</u> What There <u>Is</u> to Realize.

The "cause-and-effect" appearance of here is merely one among countless "cause-and-effect" appearances.

There are countless "worlds" of conditional appearance, of "cause-and-effect"-illusion, of ego-bondage, and of would-be seeming—all of which is, itself, the "cause" of all "effects".

You <u>become</u> the "effects".

You <u>become</u> "cause" by egoically "self"-identifying with whatever appears.

You can either egoically "self"-identify with what appears or egolessly transcend what appears.

My Divine Avataric Calling Is for you to Perfectly <u>transcend</u> what appears—no matter <u>what</u> appears.

Aham Da Asmi.

Beloved, I <u>Am</u> Da, the Self-Revelation of Reality Itself.

My Teaching <u>Is</u> Atma Nadi Shakti Dharma, the only-by-Me Divinely Avatarically Self-Revealed Transcendental Spiritual Way of Reality Itself, Which <u>Is</u> Atma Nadi Shakti Yoga, the One and Perfectly egoless Reality-Way of Adidam Ruchiradam.

I Say <u>This</u>. ■

APPENDICES

APPENDIX I

The Seven Stages of Life

His Divine Presence Ruchira Avatar Adi Da Samraj has Revealed a precise "mapping" of the developmental possibilities of human experience in the gross, subtle, and causal dimensions of the being (see glossary **gross, subtle, causal [dimensions]**). He describes these possibilities in terms of six stages of life—which account for, and correspond to, all the dimensions of experience that are potential in the human structure. His own Divine Avataric Revelation—the Realization of the "Bright", Prior to all potential experience—is the seventh stage of life. Understanding this structure of seven stages illuminates the unique nature of the process of Adidam Ruchiradam.

It is important to understand from the outset that although the numbers one to seven are a consecutive series, the seven stages of life are not. There is certainly a natural developmental relationship between the first three stages, and a kind of hierarchical and potential developmental relationship between the processes of the first six stages, so the consecutive nature of the numbers is in that sense applicable. However, in another sense, each stage is its own "universe" of experience—the world as it appears from the viewpoint of that particular stage. The six stages of human experience are like the six sides of a cube. On the cube of human potential, there are only six possible surfaces. The seventh stage of life does not appear within the human mechanism—it, instead, is the Reality-Context in which the "cube" of all the other stages appears.

The first three (or foundation) stages of life constitute the ordinary course of human adaptation—characterized (respectively) by bodily, emotional, and mental growth.

Each of the first three stages of life takes approximately seven years to be established. Every individual who lives to an adult age inevitably adapts (although, generally speaking, only partially) to the first three stages of life. In the general case, this is where the developmental potential stops—at the gross level of adaptation. Religions based fundamentally on beliefs and moral codes (without direct experience of the dimensions beyond the material world) belong to this foundation level of human development.

The fourth stage of life is characterized by a deep impulse to Communion with the Divine. It is in the context of the fourth stage of life (when one is no longer wedded to the purposes of the first three stages of life) that the true Spiritual process can begin. Throughout the history of the Great Tradition (including present time), those involved in the process of the fourth stage of life have characteristically felt the Divine to be a great "Other", in Whom they aspired to become absorbed, through devotional love and service.

Avatar Adi Da has Revealed that the full course of the true Spiritual process, beginning in the context of the fourth stage of life, involves two great dimensions—which He calls the "Vertical" and the "Horizontal". (Please see Appendix 2, "The Esoteric Anatomy of the Spiritual Process: 'Vertical' and 'Horizontal' Dimensions of the Being", p. 107.)

The descending aspect of the Vertical process characterizes the fourth stage of life, while the ascending aspect characterizes the fifth stage of life. The fifth stage process is the ascent toward absorption into the Divine Matrix of Light Infinitely Above, thereby (ultimately) Realizing the Divine as Light (or Energy) Itself. (Although this Realization is a true "taste" of the True Divine Condition, It is achieved by means of the conditional effort of ascent—and, therefore, the Realization Itself is also conditional, or non-permanent.) The fifth stage of life is the ultimate process associated with the subtle dimension of existence.

The Horizontal process characterizes the sixth stage of life. The sixth stage process is the exclusion of all awareness of the "outside" world (in both its gross and subtle dimensions), by "secluding" oneself within the heart—in order to rest in the Divine Self, Realized (ultimately) as Consciousness Itself. (Like the ultimate Realization associated with the fifth stage of life, the sixth stage Realization is also a true "taste" of the True Divine Condition. However, It is also achieved by conditional means—the conditional effort of exclusion—and, therefore, the Realization Itself is also conditional, or non-permanent.) The sixth stage of life is the process associated with the causal dimension of existence.

As Avatar Adi Da has pointed out, the typical traditional view has been that the processes of the fifth stage of life and of the sixth stage of life are <u>alternative</u> approaches to Spiritual Realization. Indeed, these approaches (of either going "Up" or going "Deep") have usually been regarded to be incompatible with each other.

In one of His summary essays about the stages of life, Avatar Adi Da discusses which traditions exemplify which stages of life:

In the Great Tradition (or common Wisdom-Inheritance) of humankind, the characteristic (or grossly ignorant) orientation of the first three stages of life (in themselves, or engaged for their own sake) is always everywhere displayed in the common "world" (to date), and every age (or epoch) displays its own unique convention (or style) of materialistic purposiveness.

In the Great Tradition of humankind, the characteristic orientation of the fourth and fifth stages of life is found (first of all) in the traditional popular "religions" (such as Hinduism, Christianity, Islam, and Judaism), and in all the esoteric traditions of fourth and fifth stage "religious" mysticism and mystical Spirituality (or descending and ascending Yoga).

In the Great Tradition of humankind, the characteristic orientation of the sixth stage of life is found in its first (or ascetical) form in such traditions as Samkhya and Jainism, and in its second (or moderate and "self"-pacifying, or "Middle Way") form principally in the traditions (or schools) of Buddhism (and also in the schools of Taoism), and in its third (or final, and Non-conditionally, or Perfectly Subjectively, Self-Affirming) form principally in the traditions (or schools) of Advaitism (or "Non-Dualism"), especially that of Advaita Vedanta (and, secondarily, or with less directness, within the schools of some varieties of Buddhism, especially within the "Mahayana" and "Vajrayana" traditions, and also, but with even less directness, within some schools of Taoism).

In the Great Tradition of humankind (previous to My Divine Avataric Appearance here), the characteristic (or Divinely, or Most Perfectly, Enlightened) "Orientation" (or "Disposition") of the seventh stage of life has not been Realized and Demonstrated. There has been occasional seeming (or suggestive) evidence, in the Teachings of a random few unique individuals and traditions—especially within the schools of Advaitism, and, secondarily (or by a less direct and characteristic expression) within some schools of Buddhism, and (but with an even less direct and characteristic expression) within some schools of Taoism—of limited foreshadowings (or partial intuitions, or insightful, but limited, premonitions) of the characteristic (or Divinely, or Most Perfectly, Enlightened) "Orientation" (or "Disposition") of the seventh stage of life. However, that evidence is only verbal, or limited to expressions of a philosophical persuasion only, and a philosophical persuasion that is (itself) founded on the sixth stage orientation, practice, and possible Realization that preceded (and still limits, in every case) the apparently "seventh stage" expression or Teaching.

—His Divine Presence
Ruchira Avatar Adi Da Samraj
"God-Talk, Real-God-Realization, Most Perfect Divine Self-Awakening, and The Seven Possible Stages of Life",
The Aletheon

The seventh stage of life, or the Realization of Avatar Adi Da's own "Bright" Divine Self-Condition, transcends the entire course of human potential. Avatar Adi Da is the Unique Revealer of the seventh stage of life. In other words, though the greatest confessions of sixth stage Realization include premonitions of the seventh stage Realization, the seventh stage of life was never, before Adi Da's Avataric Incarnation, actually Realized, Revealed, and Demonstrated. Seventh stage Realization is a profoundly "radical" turnabout relative to all the ordinary and extraordinary modes of existence that have ever been known to human beings. Therefore, the Awakening to the seventh stage Realization, on the part of Avatar Adi Da's devotees, requires practice of the "Radical" Reality-Way of Adidam Ruchiradam in its most intensive, or renunciate, form.

In the seventh stage of life, the impulse to Realize the Divine (as Light) by going "Up" and the impulse to Realize the Divine (as Consciousness) by going "Deep" are (by Avatar Adi Da's Divine Grace) simultaneously fulfilled. In that fulfillment, Avatar Adi Da Samraj Himself is most perfectly Realized. He is Realized as the "Bright", the Single Divine Unity of Consciousness and Energy—or Conscious Light Itself. This unique Realization, or Divine Enlightenment, wipes away every trace of dissociation from the body-mind and the world. There is no impulse to seek or to avoid any experience. Rather, everything that arises is Divinely Self-Recognized to be merely a modification of the Conscious Light of Reality Itself.

The seventh stage Realization is absolutely Non-conditional. In other words, it is not dependent on "conditions" of any kind, or on any form of effort by the individual. Rather, It is a Divine Gift, Given by His Divine Presence Avatar Adi Da to the devotee who has utterly surrendered all of ego to Him. Therefore, the seventh stage Realization is permanent. The seventh stage Realization, however, is not a static "finality". The process of Divine Self-Recognition itself unfolds in phases, in which the Realizer is first Transfigured and Transformed, then becomes profoundly and Divinely Indifferent to all appearances within Reality, and finally is, with the end of the physical lifetime, "Translated" beyond any possible future birth or reappearance in a limited form.

APPENDIX 2

The Esoteric Anatomy of the Spiritual Process: "Vertical" and "Horizontal" Dimensions of the Being

One of the unique aspects of Avatar Adi Da's Revelation of the "Radical" Reality-Way of Adidam Ruchiradam is His complete description of the esoteric anatomy of the human being and how this relates to the Spiritual process. Just as the human body has a gross anatomy (of bones, flesh, nerves, and so on), there is also an esoteric anatomy, consisting of three primary structures. The esoteric anatomy of the human body-mind is the basis for all dimensions of human experience—of the ordinary, extraordinary, mystical, and Transcendental kind. Understanding this esoteric anatomy is a key to understanding what makes the Reality-Way of Adidam uniquely complete, and why the Divine Enlightenment that His Divine Presence Avatar Adi Da Offers is an unprecedented Gift.

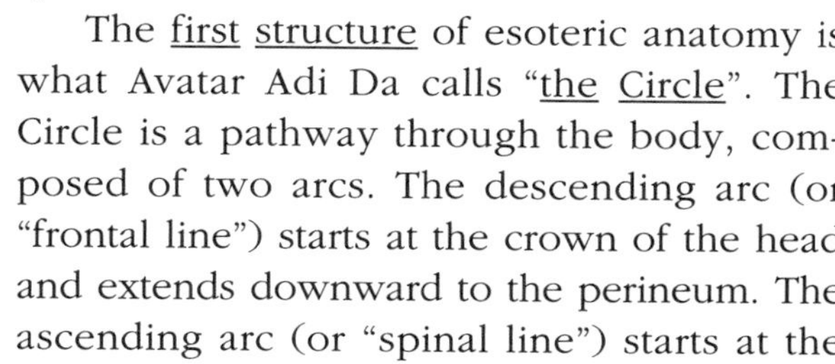

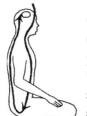

The first structure of esoteric anatomy is what Avatar Adi Da calls "the Circle". The Circle is a pathway through the body, composed of two arcs. The descending arc (or "frontal line") starts at the crown of the head and extends downward to the perineum. The ascending arc (or "spinal line") starts at the perineum and extends upward to the crown of the head. The Circle is the primary energy-pathway in the body, through which both the natural energy of life and the Divine Spirit-Energy flow. As you become more sensitive to the subtle dimensions of experience, you become capable of feeling energy moving in your body through the Circle.

The Transcendental Spiritual Initiation that Avatar Adi Da Gives to His rightly prepared First Congregation devotees is the Infusion of His Divine Transcendental Spirit-Energy (or Transcendental Spiritual Current) into the frontal line of the Circle. As you mature in the practice of Adidam, the Circle becomes more and more tangibly full of Avatar Adi Da's Divine Transcendental Spiritual Current—first in the frontal line, and then also in the spinal line. On certain occasions in the practice of a Transcendentally Spiritually mature devotee, the entire Circle will become utterly full of His Divine Transcendental Spiritual Current—so open to His Divine Infusion that one ceases to be identified with body or mind in the usual sense, and becomes aware (instead) of existing as a vastly expanded spherical form of the Divine "Brightness". This is the Samadhi of the "Thumbs"—a form of Samadhi uniquely Given by Avatar Adi Da. Eventually, the experience of the "Thumbs" becomes constant, such that the presumption of existing as body and mind no longer "rules" one's life. Then one is ready to receive Avatar Adi Da's Gift of the Awakening to the Witness-Consciousness, which makes possible the beginning of the "Perfect Practice". (See also pp. 40–43, for more about the "Thumbs".)

Because there is a "downward-and-upward" quality to the Circle (with its descending and ascending arcs), Avatar Adi Da refers to the Circle as the "Vertical" dimension of esoteric anatomy. Most of the world's Spiritual traditions are focused in processes that relate to the Circle—seeking, as an ultimate result, some kind of "ascended" Union with the Divine (found by subtly ascending beyond the body-mind, via ascent through and beyond the crown of the head). In the most advanced traditional developments of this "Vertical" approach to the Divine, there is, in fact, ascent to the Source-Matrix of Divine Light Which is Infinitely Above.

Such ascended Union with the Divine, however, is not permanent (or eternal), because it depends on the effort of the individual—the effort to "go up". Thus, such ascended Union with the Divine is not most perfect Divine Enlightenment. Rather, it is a matter of "choosing" the "Light" (or "Energy") aspect of the Divine—over the "Consciousness" aspect.

The second structure of esoteric anatomy is what Avatar Adi Da calls "the three stations of the heart". The three "stations" are:

- The "left side"—corresponding to the physical heart, and the gross dimension of the being.
- The "middle station"—corresponding to the "heart chakra" (or "anahata chakra"), and the subtle dimension of the being.
- The "right side"—which is the "seat" of the causal dimension (or "root"-dimension) of the being (equivalent to the primal presumption that one exists as a separate "self", or "ego"), and which is (simultaneously) the "doorway" in the body-mind through which the ego can be utterly dissolved, in egoless Identification with the Divine Self-Nature, Self-Condition, and Self-State of Reality Itself.

As Avatar Adi Da Says in "Atma Nadi Shakti Yoga", His Transcendental Spiritual Transmission "originates" from the Prior position, associated with the right side of the heart, and shows signs from there in the middle and left stations. In other words, His Prior Divine State manifests as Love-Bliss-Fullness pervading the causal, subtle, and gross dimensions of the being:

In the "Radical" Reality-Way of Adidam Ruchiradam, the Transcendental Spiritual Process develops via the right side of the bodily apparent heart—showing Its evidence from there to the middle station, and (then) to the left side, of the bodily apparent heart (pp. 62–63).

Because there is not a "downward-and-upward" quality to the three stations of the heart, Avatar Adi Da refers to them as the "Horizontal" dimension of esoteric anatomy. A minority of the world's Spiritual traditions (principally certain branches of the Hindu, Buddhist, Jain, and Taoist traditions) are focused in processes that relate to the Horizontal dimension (and especially the right side of the heart)—seeking, as an ultimate result, an "interiorly secluded" Identification with the Divine (or Realization of Truth). In the fullest development of this "Horizontal" approach, the practitioner does, in fact, experience an Identification with the Divine (or a Realization of Truth) that is achieved by excluding all awareness of body and mind and world. Such exclusionary Union with the Divine, however, is not permanent (or eternal), because it depends on the effort of the individual—the effort to "go within", or to exclude everything that is apparently objective. Thus, such exclusionary Union with the Divine is not most perfect Divine Enlightenment. Rather, it is a matter of "choosing" the "Consciousness" aspect of the Divine—over the "Light" (or "Energy") aspect.

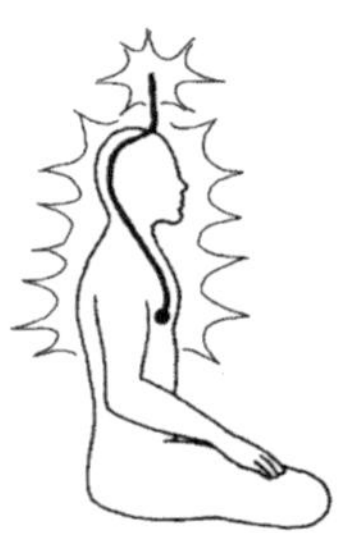

The third (and quintessential) structure of esoteric anatomy is what Avatar Adi Da calls, using traditional Sanskrit terms, "Atma Nadi" (meaning "Heart-Current of the Transcendental Self-State"), or (alternatively) "Amrita Nadi" (meaning "Channel of Spiritual Nectar"). Atma Nadi is a radiant energy-structure, the "Bright" Itself as It Manifests in the context of the human body-mind. Atma Nadi is shaped like the letter "S", extending from the right side of the heart (as its "lower terminal") through the chest, throat, and head, and then to the Source-Matrix of Divine Light Infinitely Above (as its "upper terminal"). Thus, Atma Nadi encompasses both of the "locations" that have (in the most esoteric branches of the Great Tradition) been sought as the ultimate Divine "place"—the infinitely ascended Matrix of Light ("Above") and the right side of the heart ("within", or, more accurately, "Prior").

In the Great Tradition of religion and Spirituality, there have been two fundamental "camps"—the "Vertical" and the "Horizontal", or those who seek the Divine by going "up" and those who seek the Divine by going "within". What makes Avatar Adi Da's Revelation of the "Radical" Reality-Way of Adidam Ruchiradam utterly unique is His "Disclosure" that, although both the Vertical and the Horizontal approaches are capable of resulting in a true glimpse of the Divine (or of Perfect Truth), neither the Vertical nor the Horizontal approach can lead to most perfect Divine Enlightenment (which is permanent, or eternal). Only the simultaneous Realization of the Divine in both "locations"—the infinitely ascended Source-Matrix of Divine Light and the right side of the heart (or both "terminals" of Atma Nadi)—is Most Perfect (and Eternal) Divine Enlightenment. Only the Full and Indivisible Realization of the Divine as Conscious Light (Consciousness and Light) is Most Perfect (and Eternal) Divine Enlightenment. Such is the infinitely glorious Realization Given by Avatar Adi Da to His devotees who complete the entire process of the Reality-Way of Adidam. That Realization has never been known before Avatar Adi Da's Appearance in the world and His Gift of the Reality-Way of Adidam. Such is the culmination of the searchless process of simply Beholding His Divine Presence Avatar Adi Da, the bodily (human) Incarnation of the "Bright" Itself.

Thus, Adidam is neither a "Vertical" way nor a "Horizontal" way. Rather, it is the unique "Vertical-and-Horizontal" Way. It is the "Radical" Reality-Way of whole bodily Enlightenment, because it culminates in the Most Perfect Realization of the "whole body" of Atma Nadi.

APPENDIX 3

The Three Dimensions of Adidam Ruchiradam

Avatar Adi Da Samraj has described three foundation dimensions of the "Radical" Reality-Way of Adidam Ruchiradam. Even from the earliest moment of the embrace of the Reality-Way of Adidam, these three characteristics of practice are both the means and the demonstration of the transcending of ego (or transcending identification with the separate body-mind-self) in devotional Communion with His Divine Presence Ruchira Avatar Adi Da Samraj.

THE FIRST DIMENSION

"Radical" Devotion

The Root-Practice of Heart-Beholding His Divine Presence Ruchira Avatar Adi Da Samraj As Reality Itself

The foundation of the Reality-Way of Adidam is **"radical" devotion** to Ruchira Avatar Adi Da Samraj, Who is recognized at heart to be the Revelation of Reality Itself in human form. Such devotion is "radical" because it is a response to Avatar Adi Da's Revelation with every faculty of the body and mind, resonant with Him at the very "root" of the being, prior to the presumption of a separate self. Once practice of devotional turning to Him is rightly established, it becomes a moment to moment devotional Communion that Avatar Adi Da calls "searchless Beholding" of Him.

THE SECOND DIMENSION

Right Life

Re-patterning the Energies of the Total Body-Mind

In the context of heart-response to Avatar Adi Da Samraj, the devotee lives a comprehensive discipline of **right life** based on the non-seeking disposition Revealed in devotional Communion with Him. This includes specific practices relative to all aspects of practical and relational life—including money, food, sexuality, and social relations—as well as a sacred life of meditation, worship, and service in cooperative association with other devotees of Avatar Adi Da Samraj. This life purifies, balances, and rejuvenates the body-mind in the equanimity of Communion with Avatar Adi Da Samraj.

THE THIRD DIMENSION

"Perfect Knowledge"

Priorly Standing in the egoless Reality-Position

On the foundation of devotional response to Him and the living of right life, Avatar Adi Da Samraj Calls His devotee to "consider" and be established in the **"Perfect Knowledge"** of Reality Itself. This is engaged first via a "preliminary" practice—and ultimately, for mature practitioners, via a "Perfect Practice"—of "Perfect Knowledge". In Communion with Avatar Adi Da, He Reveals that no "object" or "knowledge" or "subject" or "point of view" is True or Real—but, rather, Reality Itself is Shown as the Prior and egoless Condition that is Always Already the Case.

"Radical" devotion to Me is right and true devotional recognition of Me, always responsively whole bodily turning to Me and searchlessly "self"-surrendering to Me—on Sight.

Right life is straightforward obedience to Me, without reservations (or "looking right and left").

The preliminary practice of "Perfect Knowledge" is the attentive Listening to My Divine Avataric Revelation-Instruction relative to Reality Itself—Which Is Always Already The (One and Only) Case, and Which Is Self-Evidently Divine (As Is).

"Radical" devotion to Me, right life, and "Perfect Knowledge" are—all three—implicit (or Always Already Given, by and As Me) in right and true devotional (and, in due course, Transcendental Spiritual) Communion with Me (As I Am).

—His Divine Presence Ruchira Avatar Adi Da Samraj
"Acausal Adidam",
The Aletheon

APPENDIX 4

The Congregations of Adidam Ruchiradam

In order to make it possible for all kinds of people to formally relate to Him, His Divine Presence Ruchira Avatar Adi Da Samraj has created four "congregations" of the Reality-Way of Adidam. The congregations radiate like a mandala, or sacred pattern, from Adi Da Samraj at its heart.

■ The **First Congregation** comprises those devotees who engage the full and intensive process of "radical" devotion, right life, and "Perfect Knowledge" in the Reality-Way of Adidam—first as student-beginners, and then accepted into the Transcendental Spiritual process, and Awakening, ultimately, to Divine Self-Realization.

■ The **Second Congregation** comprises the gathering of Avatar Adi Da's devotees who engage the foundational process of "radical" devotion, right life, and "Perfect Knowledge".

■ The **Third Congregation** comprises the supportive gathering of those who respond to Avatar Adi Da Samraj and are moved to embrace a simple practice of "radical" devotion to Him and support of His Work. The third congregation also includes individuals who maintain a traditional religious affiliation, while also embracing the supportive obligations of this congregation.

■ The **Fourth Congregation** comprises those from indigenous and traditional cultures around the world who devotionally respond to Avatar Adi Da Samraj and are moved to embrace a simple life of practice in relation to Him.

Beyond the congregations of Adidam stand many who respond to Avatar Adi Da Samraj, and who choose to study or assist His Work without formally becoming His devotees.

"Atma Nadi Shakti Yoga" is a specific address to the full Real-God-Realizing process of the Reality-Way of Adidam, which is demonstrated in the context of the First Congregation of Adidam. The essay also addresses practice in the Second Congregation as necessary preparation for entrance into the First Congregation.

APPENDIX 5

Forms of Samadhi Unique to Adidam and Traditional Forms of Samadhi

The Sanskrit word "Samadhi" traditionally denotes various exalted states that appear in the context of esoteric meditation and Realization. Avatar Adi Da Teaches that, for His devotees, Samadhi is, even more simply and fundamentally, the Enjoyment of His Divine State (or "Divine Samadhi"), Which is experienced (even from the beginning of the practice of Adidam) through ego-transcending devotional Communion with Him. However, additionally there are specific processes and events that can be called forms of "Samadhi" in the "Radical" Reality-Way of Adidam Ruchiradam.

In "Atma Nadi Shakti Yoga", His Divine Presence Avatar Adi Da Samraj contrasts the egoless manifestations of the Samadhi of the "Thumbs" and seventh stage Sahaja Nirvikalpa Samadhi with traditional forms of Samadhi (Savikalpa Samadhi and fifth stage conditional Nirvikalpa Samadhi) that are based on the platform of the body-mind-complex.

Forms of Samadhi Unique to the Reality-Way of Adidam

There are two forms of Samadhi that are unique to the Reality-Way of Adidam.

Samadhi of the "Thumbs"—"The 'Thumbs'" is Avatar Adi Da's technical term for the Invasion of the body-mind by a particular form of the forceful Descent of His Divine Transcendental Spiritual Current.

In the fullest form of this experience, which Avatar Adi Da calls "the Samadhi of the 'Thumbs'", His Spirit-Invasion Descends all the way to the bottom of the frontal line of the body-mind (at the bodily base) and ascends through the spinal line, overwhelming the ordinary human sense of bodily existence, infusing the whole being with intense blissfulness, and releasing the ordinary, confined sense of body, mind, and separate "self" in His Prior State.

In this "Samadhi of the 'Thumbs'", there is a profound turnabout in the devotee's awareness of Avatar Adi Da Samraj. While still always turning to Him devotionally in His bodily (human) Divine Form, the devotee begins to recognize Him as Consciousness Itself—the "Root"-Position of existence, Prior to all that is arising in body, mind, and world. This recognition is Transcendentally Spiritually established—and it is the basis for making a profound shift, away from identification with the body-mind and to the transition to the "Perfect Practice" of the Reality-Way of Adidam.

Eventually, in what Avatar Adi Da calls the "'Radical' Self-Manifestation of the 'Thumbs'", this process leads to the stable Awakening of the Witness-Consciousness and the transition to the "Perfect Practice" of Adidam. See pp. 40–43 for Avatar Adi Da's description of the "Thumbs" in this essay.

Avatar Adi Da's Revelation-Gift of the "Thumbs" is unique to the Reality-Way of Adidam, for it is a specific manifestation of the "Crashing Down" (or the Divine Descent) of Avatar Adi Da's Spirit-Baptism, into the body-minds of His devotees. The Samadhi of the "Thumbs" is a kind of "Nirvikalpa" (or formless) Samadhi—but in descent in the frontal line, rather than in ascent in the spinal line.

Non-conditional (or seventh stage) Sahaja Nirvikalpa Samadhi—The Sanskrit term "Nirvikalpa Samadhi" literally means "meditative ecstasy without form", or "deep meditative concentration (or absorption) in which there is no perception of form (or defined experiential content)". "Sahaja" is Sanskrit for "innate, or natural". Thus, "Sahaja Nirvikalpa Samadhi" means "Innate formless Samadhi". Sahaja Nirvikalpa Samadhi is the full demonstration of the Awakening in the seventh stage of life (see Appendix 1, p. 101), and it is Non-conditional, or not based on any conditions in the body-mind-complex.

This "Samadhi", Demonstrated for the first time through the Avataric Life of Adi Da Samraj, is not based on any form of withdrawal from conditions and relations. Rather, it is the most Sublime and Profound Demonstration of Love-Bliss. In Avatar Adi Da's Words, the world is "Divinely Self-Recognized", or tacitly comprehended, as a modification of the Conscious Light of Reality, and not "different" from It. Everything conditional—everything material, everything subtle or psychic, even attention itself—is Realized to Be Conscious Light. Once truly Realized, seventh stage Sahaja Nirvikalpa Samadhi is Just So, and that Freedom cannot be lost.

In seventh stage Sahaja Nirvikalpa Samadhi, the One and Only (Transcendental, Inherently Spiritual, Inherently Indivisible, Intrinsically egoless, Perfectly Acausal, Perfectly Transcendental Spiritual, and Self-Evidently Divine) Conscious Light Merely Self-Abides—Always With "Open Eyes", Merely Present (or Self-Awakened, and Self-Aware) As Itself.

—His Divine Presence Ruchira Avatar Adi Da Samraj
The Aletheon

Traditional Forms of Samadhi

There are also several traditional manifestations of Samadhi discussed in this essay.

fifth stage conditional (or conditionally ascended, or Fully Ascended) Nirvikalpa Samadhi—The Sanskrit term "Nirvikalpa Samadhi" literally means "meditative ecstasy without form", or "deep meditative concentration (or absorption) in which there is no perception of form (or defined experiential content)". Traditionally, this state is regarded to be the final goal of the many schools of Yogic ascent whose orientation to practice is that of the fifth stage of life. Fifth stage conditional Nirvikalpa Samadhi is an isolated or periodic (and, necessarily, temporary) Realization. In it, attention ascends beyond all conditional manifestation into the formless Matrix of Divine Vibration and Divine Light Infinitely Above the world, the body, and the mind. It is produced by manipulation of attention and of the body-mind, and is (therefore) incapable of being maintained when attention returns (as it inevitably does) to the states of the body-mind. In the Reality-Way of Adidam, conditionally ascended Nirvikalpa Samadhi is a possible, but not necessary, experience.

In "Atma Nadi Shakti Yoga", Avatar Adi Da references the Event in His own "Sadhana Years" in which He "Experienced" Nirvikalpa Samadhi in what He describes as its "Priorly Ascended" form—a Unique Sign of His Divine Avataric Nature.

Savikalpa Samadhi—The Sanskrit term "Savikalpa Samadhi" literally means "meditative ecstasy with form", or "deep meditative concentration (or absorption) in which form (or defined experiential content) is still perceived". Avatar Adi Da indicates that there are two basic forms of Savikalpa Samadhi. The first is characterized by the various experiences produced by the Spiritual ascent of energy and attention (into mystical phenomena, visions, and other subtle sensory perceptions of subtle psychic forms) and the various states of Yogic Bliss (or Spirit-"Intoxication").

The second (and highest) form of Savikalpa Samadhi is called "Cosmic Consciousness", or the "'Vision' of Cosmic Unity". This is an isolated or periodic occurrence in which attention ascends, uncharacteristically and spontaneously, to a state of awareness wherein conditional existence is perceived as a Unity in Divine Awareness. The experience of "Cosmic Consciousness" is pursued as the ultimate goal of certain mystical and Yogic paths. It depends upon manipulation of attention and the body-mind, and it is interpreted from the "point of view" of the separate (body-based or mind-based) self—and, therefore, it is not equivalent to Divine Enlightenment. In the Reality-Way of Adidam Ruchiradam, the various forms of Savikalpa Samadhi may be experienced, but none of them are necessary to the process of Adidam.

GLOSSARY

Adidam / Adidam Ruchiradam—When His Divine Presence Ruchira Avatar Adi Da Samraj spontaneously Gave the name "Adidam" (in January 1996) to the Reality-Way He has Revealed, He pointed out that the name "Adidam" evokes His Primal Self-Confession, "I Am Adi Da", or, more simply, "I Am Da".

"Ruchiradam" is a word newly coined by Avatar Adi Da, deriving from Sanskrit "Ruchira" (meaning "bright" or "radiant"). The compound reference "Adidam Ruchiradam" communicates that Adidam is the Way of devotion to Avatar Adi Da Samraj—Who Is the "Bright" Itself, and Who Gives the Realization of His own "Bright" Self-Condition. Furthermore, "Ruchira Dham Hermitage" is the name Avatar Adi Da gave to the place where He underwent a profound and unprecedented Yogic Event that marked the Perfection of His Revelation of the "Radical" Reality-Way of Adidam Ruchiradam. Thus, the name Adidam Ruchiradam honors that Event.

Aham Da Asmi—Sanskrit phrase meaning "I (Aham) Am (Asmi) Da". Avatar Adi Da's Avatarically Self-Revealed Divine Name, "Da" (meaning "the One Who Gives"), indicates that Avatar Adi Da Samraj is the Supreme Divine Giver, the Avataric Incarnation of the Very Divine Person.

all-and-All—A phrase His Divine Presence Ruchira Avatar Adi Da Samraj has created to describe the totality of conditional (or ordinarily appearing) existence—both as the "sum of its parts" and as an undivided whole. He defines lowercase "all" as indicating "the collected sum of all presumed-to-be-separate beings, things, and conditions", and uppercase "All" as indicating "the All (or the undivided totality) of conditional existence as a whole".

Amrita Nadi—a term synonymous with **Atma Nadi**. "Amrita Nadi" is Sanskrit for "Channel of Spiritual Nectar".

Arrow—In deep meditation, Avatar Adi Da's Avatarically Self-Transmitted Divine Transcendental Spiritual Current may be felt in the form of the Arrow (which Avatar Adi Da defines as "The breathless and Moveless, but Upwardly Polarized, Central Axis . . . Of the Cosmically-Patterned body-mind"), rather than in the form of the Circle (in which the natural life-energy and—in the case of Transcendentally Spiritually Awakened practitioners of Adidam—Avatar Adi Da's Divine Transcendental Spiritual Energy are felt to circulate down the frontal line and up the spinal line). See also Appendix 2.

Atma Bindu—In Sanskrit, "bindu" means "point" or "source"; "atma" means the supreme "Self". Avatar Adi Da defines "Atma Bindu" in this essay as "the egoless 'Root-Point', or Source-'Point', or Heart-'Root' of Consciousness Itself, At, and Always Perfectly Prior to, the right side of the bodily apparent heart".

Atma Nadi—Atma Nadi is Sanskrit for "Heart-Current of the Transcendental Self-State". Atma Nadi (or, alternatively, Amrita Nadi) is the ultimate "root"-structure of the body-mind, Realized as such in the seventh stage of life in the "Radical" Reality-Way of Adidam Ruchiradam.

Atma Nadi Shakti Dharma—The Transcendental Spiritual (Shakti) Teaching (Dharma) of the Atma Nadi (the Perfectly egoless Heart-Current of the Transcendental Self-State). A descriptive reference to Avatar Adi Da's Revelation of the "Radical" Reality-Way of Adidam Ruchiradam.

Atma Nadi Shakti Yoga—The Transcendental Spiritual (Shakti) process (Yoga) of the Atma Nadi (the Perfectly egoless Heart-Current of the Transcendental Self-State). A descriptive reference to the "Radical" Reality-Way of Adidam Ruchiradam, particularly as it is demonstrated in the First Congregation of Adidam.

bodily base—A phrase Avatar Adi Da uses to refer to the region that includes the genitals, the perineum, and the anus.

"Bright"—By the word "Bright" (and its variations, such as "Brightness"), Avatar Adi Da refers to the Self-Existing and Self-Radiant Divine Reality that He has Revealed since His Birth. Avatar Adi Da named His own Self-Evidently Divine Self-Condition "the 'Bright'" in His Infancy, as soon as He acquired the capability of language.

This term is placed in quotation marks to indicate that His Divine Presence Avatar Adi Da uses it with the specific meaning described here.

the "Circle"—See Appendix 2.

"conductivity"—Avatar Adi Da's technical term for participation in (and responsibility for) the movement of natural bodily energies via intentional exercises of feeling and breathing. Such exercises include all of the searchless right-life disciplines Given by Avatar Adi Da to His devotees—such as the raw diet, meditation, "conscious exercise", emotional-sexual practices, sacramental worship, devotional service, etc. When Avatar Adi Da's devotee is Transcendentally Spiritually Awakened by Him, the devotee practices "Transcendental Spirit-'conductivity'"—or participation in and responsibility for the movement of Avatar Adi Da's Divine Transcendental Spiritual Current of Love-Bliss in its natural course of association with the body-mind-complex. (Avatar Adi Da's principal Instruction relative to the "general" or "basic" forms of Transcendental Spirit-"conductivity" is Given in *The Dawn Horse Testament*.) The term "conductivity" is placed in quotation marks to indicate that Avatar Adi Da uses it with the specific technical meaning described here.

congregations of Adidam Ruchiradam—See Appendix 4.

Cosmic Mandala—The Sanskrit word "mandala" (literally, "circle") is commonly used in the esoteric Spiritual traditions of the East to describe the hierarchical levels of cosmic existence. "Mandala" also denotes an artistic rendering of a visionary representation of the cosmos. Avatar Adi Da uses the phrase "Cosmic Mandala" as a reference to the totality of the conditionally manifested cosmos (or all worlds, forms, and beings), which (He has Revealed) can be visually perceived (and, thus, represented) as a pattern of concentric circular bands (or, more accurately, spheres) of certain distinct colors (each of a particular relative width), with a Brilliant White Five-Pointed Star at the center.

Crashing Down—Avatar Adi Da's Divine Spirit-Force "Descending Utterly, From The 'Place' Infinitely Above the body-mind and the world, Down and Most Deeply Into the body-mind and the world—Even To The Degree That the ego-'I', or 'self'-Contraction, Is Utterly Confounded, Utterly Yielded, and Utterly Vanished In My Avatarically Self-Revealed, and Self-Evidently Divine, Person, or Self-Condition, Which Is Real Acausal God, and Truth, and Reality" [*The Dawn Horse Testament*].

Avatar Adi Da underscores the primary importance of His Crashing Down by Confessing that, "My Divine Avataric Transcendental Spiritual Work (Altogether) Is My Crashing-Down Descent, At First Upon and Into My Own Avatarically-Born Bodily (Human) Divine Form, and, Thereafter (and Now, and Forever Hereafter), Upon and Into the body-minds Of My Devotees and all beings—Even (By Means Of My Divine Avataric Embrace Of each, and all, and All) To Infuse and (At Last) To Divinely Translate each, and all, and All" [*The Dawn Horse Testament*].

Da—Avatar Adi Da's Divine Name "Da" means "The One Who Gives", or "The Divine Giver". This Name was spontaneously Revealed to Avatar Adi Da as His Principal Divine Name—and it is a syllable with great sacred significance in various cultures. Tibetan Buddhists regard the syllable "Da" (written, in Tibetan, with a single symbol) as most auspicious, and they assign numerous sacred meanings to it, including "Entrance into the Dharma". In the most ancient of the Upanishads (the *Brihadaranyaka Upanishad*), the Divine Being gives the fundamental instruction necessary for each of the different classes of living beings by uttering the single sound "Da". (Each class of beings understands "Da" in the manner uniquely necessary in their case.) In this passage, "Da" is said to be the Divine Voice that can be heard speaking through thunder (S. Radhakrishnan, trans., *The Principal Upanishads* [Atlantic Highlands, N.J.: Humanities Press International, First paperback ed., 1992], 289–90).

"difference"—Avatar Adi Da Samraj defines the presumption of fundamental "difference" as the essential fault that characterizes the unliberated human ego. The core of this presumption is the primal notion that "self" is separate from "everything and everyone else". That primal notion is described by Avatar Adi Da as the "root" of all human suffering and dilemma.

Divine Avataric Acausal Self-"Emergence"—On January 11, 1986, Avatar Adi Da passed through a profound Yogic Swoon, Which He later described as the Yogic Establishment of His Divine Avataric Acausal Self-"Emergence". Avatar Adi Da's Divine Avataric Acausal Self-"Emergence" is an ongoing Process in which His Avatarically-Born bodily (human) Divine Form has been (and is ever more profoundly and potently being) Conformed to Himself, the Very Divine Person, such that His bodily (human) Form is now (and forever hereafter) an utterly Unobstructed Sign and Agent of His Own Divine Being. For Avatar Adi Da's extended description of His Divine Avataric Acausal Self-"Emergence", see Part Three of *The Knee of Listening*.

Divine Indifference—See **four phases of the seventh stage of life**.

Divine Translation—See **four phases of the seventh stage of life**.

Divinely Self-Recognized—See **Self-Abiding Divine Self-Recognition**.

ego-"I"—The presumption of separate and separative existence. The "I" is placed in quotation marks to indicate that it is used by Avatar Adi Da in the "so to speak" sense. He is communicating (by means of the quotation marks) that, in reality, there is no such thing as the separate "I", even though it appears to be the case from the "point of view" of ordinary human perception.

fifth stage conditional Nirvikalpa Samadhi—See Appendix 5.

First Congregation—See Appendix 4.

four phases of the seventh stage of life—Avatar Adi Da has Revealed that the Awakening to the seventh stage of life—or Divine Enlightenment—is not an "endpoint" but is (rather) the beginning of the final Transcendental Spiritual process. One of the unique aspects of Avatar Adi Da's Revelation is His precise description of the seventh stage process as consisting of four phases: Divine Transfiguration, Divine Transformation, Divine Indifference, and Divine Translation.

> *The First Sign (or Demonstration) Of The Only-By-Me Revealed and Given Seventh Stage Of Life (In The "Radical" Reality-Way Of The Heart) Is Divine Transfiguration, In Which the body-mind Of My . . . Devotee Is Self-Radiant With My Avatarically Self-Transmitted Divine Love-Bliss, Spontaneously Blessing all of the (Apparent) relations of the body-mind.*
>
> *The Second Sign (or Demonstration) Of The Only-By-Me Revealed and Given Seventh Stage Of Life (In The "Radical" Reality-Way Of The Heart) Is Divine Transformation, In Which the body-mind Of My . . . Devotee Effectively Exhibits The Only-By-Me Revealed and Given Signs and Powers Of Real (Acausal) God.*
>
> *The Third Sign (or Demonstration) Of The Only-By-Me Revealed and Given Seventh Stage Of Life (In The "Radical" Reality-Way Of The Heart) Is Divine Indifference, In Which Even the body-mind Of My . . . Devotee Is Pre-Occupied With The Self-Existing Event Of My Self-Radiant Love-Bliss, and the "world" of (Apparent) relations Is (More and More) Minimally and Not Otherwise Noticed. . . .*
>
> *The Final Sign (or Demonstration) Of The Only-By-Me Revealed and Given Seventh Stage Of Life (and Of The Total Practice Of The Only-By-Me Revealed and Given "Radical" Reality-Way Of The Heart) Is The Great Event Of Divine Translation—Which Is . . . The Process Of Transition To (or "Dawning" As) My Divine Self-Domain Via The Divinely "Bright" Outshining Of The Cosmic Domain In The Only-By-Me Revealed and Given Divine Sphere and Sign Of The "Midnight Sun" (Most Perfectly Beyond and Prior To all-and-All Of Cosmic, or conditional, forms, beings, signs, conditions, relations, and things).*
>
> —His Divine Presence Ruchira Avatar Adi Da Samraj
> *The Dawn Horse Testament*

"Four Thorns of Heart-Instruction"—The core Text of Avatar Adi Da's Instruction on the Transcendental Spiritual process in *Hridaya Rosary* (The Dawn Horse Press, 2005).

frontal line—See Appendix 2.

fully adapted student-beginner—See **student-beginner**.

"great path of return"—Avatar Adi Da characterizes the traditional religious, Spiritual, and Transcendental paths of the first six stages of life as the "great path of return" because the traditional points of view associated with the first six stages of life regard the "goal" of the Spiritual path to be somewhere "else" than "here". In other words, it is traditionally presumed that the Spiritual Way is a matter of following a "great path" by which the aspirant will "return" from "here" to the "place" that is regarded to be the "goal" (or "home").

Right practice of the "Radical" Reality-Way of Adidam Ruchiradam, on the other hand, is not a matter of seeking to reach any of the "goals" of the first six stages of life, but is (rather) a matter of practicing (always directly, or with always immediate effectiveness) "radical" (or priorly ego-transcending) devotion to Avatar Adi Da, while persistently observing, understanding, and transcending all forms of motivated seeking as they arise.

This term is placed in quotation marks to indicate that His Divine Presence Avatar Adi Da uses it with the specific technical meaning described here.

Great Tradition—The "Great Tradition" is Avatar Adi Da's term for the total inheritance of human, cultural, religious, magical, mystical, Spiritual, and Transcendental paths, philosophies, and testimonies, from all the eras and cultures of humanity—which inheritance has (in the present era of worldwide communication) become the common legacy of humankind.

gross, subtle, causal (dimensions)—Avatar Adi Da (in agreement with certain esoteric schools) describes conditional existence as having three fundamental dimensions—gross, subtle, and causal.

"Gross" means "made up of material (or physical) elements". The gross (or physical) dimension is, therefore, associated with the physical body. The gross dimension is also associated with experience in the waking state and, as Avatar Adi Da reveals, with the frontal line of the body-mind and with the left side of the heart (or the gross physical heart).

The subtle dimension, which is senior to and pervades the gross dimension, consists of the etheric (or personal life-energy) functions, the lower mental functions (including the conscious mind, the subconscious mind, and the unconscious mind) and higher mental functions (of discriminative mind, mentally presumed egoity, and will), and is associated with experience in the dreaming state. In the human psycho-physical structure, the subtle dimension is primarily associated with the middle station of the heart (or the heart chakra), the spinal line, the brain core, and the subtle centers of mind in the higher brain.

The causal dimension is senior to both the gross and the subtle dimensions. It is the "root" of attention, or the "root"-sense of existence as a separate "self". The causal dimension is associated with the right side of the bodily apparent heart, specifically with the sinoatrial node, or "pacemaker" (the psycho-physical source of the heartbeat). Its corresponding state of consciousness is the formless awareness of deep sleep.

Hearing—See **Listening, Hearing, Seeing**.

horizontal dimension—See Appendix 2.

Kundalini / Kundalini Shakti—The energy traditionally viewed to lie dormant at the base of the spine, associated with the muladhara chakra, or lowermost psychic center of the body-mind.

"late-time" (or "dark" epoch)—Avatar Adi Da Samraj uses the term "late-time" or "'dark' epoch" to describe the present era—in which doubt of anything at all beyond mortal existence is more and more pervading the entire world, and the interest of the separate individual "self" is more and more regarded to be the ultimate principle of life.

Listening, Hearing, Seeing—Avatar Adi Da describes the entire course of the "Radical" Reality-Way of Adidam Ruchiradam as falling into four primary phases:

1. Sighting and Listening to Him
2. Hearing Him
3. Seeing Him
4. the "Perfect Practice" of egolessly Self-Identifying with Him.

Avatar Adi Da's technical term for the course of preparatory practice in the "Radical" Reality-Way of Adidam Ruchiradam is "Sighting Him and Listening to Him". The beginner's practice is engaged entirely in the context of devotional "Sighting" of Avatar Adi Da—via regular regard of His human Body in representational Form, or via broadcasts of Him via the Internet, or in His physical Company (on special pilgrimage retreats engaged by qualified devotees). Beginning devotees listen to recitations of Avatar Adi Da's Word as often as possible, and also to the telling of the Leelas (or stories) of His Life and Work. Avatar Adi Da places particular importance on the practice of listening to the recitation of His "Perfect Knowledge" Teachings, as Given in "The Teaching Manual of Perfect Summaries". Additionally, beginning devotees study His Instruction altogether and apply it in daily life. Thus, the "Sighting and Listening" process includes (1) establishment of the fundamental practice of "radical" devotion, (2) adaptation to the supportive practice of right-life discipline, and (3) listening to Avatar Adi Da's "Perfect Knowledge" Teachings. This becomes a demonstration of true balance in the being—which comes with the establishment of the devotional practice of turning the faculties to Avatar Adi Da Samraj—or the equanimity of searchless Beholding of Him.

Once the foundation practice is fully established, the devotee applies to come on extended formal retreat in Avatar Adi Da's physical Company (or, after His physical Lifetime, in the physical company, and the by-Him-Transcendentally-Spiritually-Empowered circumstances, of the Ruchira Sannyasin Order of Adidam Ruchiradam). In the retreat circumstance, when the rightly prepared devotee truly (whole bodily) turns the principal faculties to Him, Avatar Adi Da is spontaneously Moved to Grant His

Transcendental Spiritual Initiation (or Ruchira Shaktipat), such that the devotee can become more and more consistently capable of tangibly "Locating" and "Knowing" His Divine Avataric Transcendental Spiritual Self-Transmission. This is the beginning of the Transcendentally-Spiritually-Awakened practice of the "Radical" Reality-Way of Adidam Ruchiradam—when the devotional relationship to Avatar Adi Da becomes (by His Divine Avataric Spiritual Grace) the devotional-and-Transcendental-Spiritual relationship to Him. The phase of Listening to Avatar Adi Da, rightly and effectively engaged, eventually culminates (by His Divine Avataric Spiritual Grace) in the true Hearing of Him. The devotee has begun to Hear Avatar Adi Da when there is most fundamental understanding of the "root"-act of egoity (or "self"-contraction), or the unique capability to consistently transcend the "self"-contraction. The capability of true Hearing is not something the ego can "achieve". That capability can only be Granted, by Means of Avatar Adi Da's Divine Avataric Transcendental Spiritual Grace, to His devotee who has effectively completed the (eventually, Transcendentally Spiritually Awakened) process of Listening.

When Spiritually Awakened practice of the "Radical" Reality-Way of Adidam Ruchiradam is magnified by means of the hearing-capability, the devotee has the necessary preparation to (in due course) engage that Transcendentally Spiritually Awakened practice in the "fully technically responsible" manner. This is another point (in the course of the Way of Adidam) when the devotee engages an extended formal retreat in Avatar Adi Da's physical Company (or, after His physical Lifetime, in the physical company, and the by-Him-Transcendentally-Spiritually-Empowered circumstances, of the Ruchira Sannyasin Order of Adidam Ruchiradam). In this case, in Response to the devotee's more mature practice of devotional and Transcendental Spiritual resort to Him, Avatar Adi Da Gives the Initiatory Transcendental Spiritual Gift of Upward-turned Transcendental Spiritual "Locating" and "Knowing" of Him (as He describes in this essay, and more fully in *Hridaya Rosary*). This is Avatar Adi Da's Transcendental Spiritual Initiation of His devotee into the Seeing phase of practice, which Avatar Adi Da describes as the "fully technically responsible" form of Transcendentally Spiritually Awakened Communion with Him.

As the process of Seeing develops, the whole body becomes more and more fully Infused by Avatar Adi Da's Transcendental Spirit-Baptism, purified of any psycho-physical patterning that diminishes that reception. With increasing maturity in the Seeing process, Avatar Adi Da's Transmission of the "Bright" is experienced in the unique form that He describes as "the 'Thumbs'" (see pp. 40–43)—and, through this process, the devotee is gracefully grown entirely beyond egoic "self"-identification with the body-mind-complex. The Seeing process is complete when the devotee receives Avatar Adi Da's Gift of Transcendentally Spiritually Awakening as the Witness-Consciousness (That Stands Prior to body, mind, and world, and even the act of attention itself). This Awakening to the Witness-Consciousness marks readiness for another period of Initiatory retreat in Avatar Adi Da's physical Company (or, after His physical Lifetime, in the physical company, and the by-Him-Transcendentally-Spiritually-Empowered circumstances, of the Ruchira Sannyasin Order of Adidam Ruchiradam), in which He Spiritually Initiates the devotee into the "Perfect Practice".

"Locate"—To "Locate" Avatar Adi Da is to "Truly Heart-Find" Him. Avatar Adi Da places this term (and its variants) in quotation marks to indicate the sense of "so to speak"—because He is, in reality, Omnipresent, without any specific "location".

Maha-Bindu—In the esoteric Yogic traditions of India, the Sanskrit word "bindu" (literally, "drop" or "point") suggests that all manifested forms, energies, and universes are ultimately coalesced or expressed in a point without spatial or temporal dimension. Each level (or plane) of psycho-physical reality (gross, subtle, and causal) is said to have a corresponding Maha-bindu (or zero-point). Avatar Adi Da's description of the "True 'Maha-Bindu'" (or the "'Zero point' . . . of Origin") is given on pp. 45–46.

"Midnight Sun"—A term Avatar Adi Da uses to refer to His Revelation of the esoteric visionary representation of Reality as a White Sphere in a black field—which Sphere is His own Divine Form.

Avatar Adi Da places this term in quotation marks to indicate that He uses it with the specific technical meaning described here (rather than any other more common general meaning).

Most Perfect(ly) / Most Ultimate(ly)—Avatar Adi Da uses the phrase "Most Perfect(ly)" in the sense of "Absolutely Perfect(ly)". Similarly, the phrase "Most Ultimate(ly)" is equivalent to "Absolutely Ultimate(ly)". "Most Perfect(ly)" and "Most Ultimate(ly)" are always references to the seventh (or Divinely Enlightened) stage of life. Avatar Adi Da uses "Perfect(ly)" and "Ultimate(ly)" (without "Most") to refer to the practice and realization in the context of the "Perfect Practice" of the "Radical" Reality-Way of Adidam Ruchiradam (or, when making reference to other traditions, to practice and realization in the context of the sixth stage of life).

Non-conditional (or seventh stage) Sahaja Nirvikalpa Samadhi—See Appendix 5.

"object" / "objective"—Avatar Adi Da Samraj consistently places the words "object", "objective", and so forth, in quotation marks. He does this in order to indicate that, in Reality Itself, there is no such thing as an "object" that is separate from the "subject".

Outshined—"Outshine" and its variants refer to the process of Divine Translation, the final Demonstration of the four-phase process of the seventh stage of life in the "Radical" Reality-Way of Adidam Ruchiradam. In the Great Event of Outshining (or Divine Translation), body, mind, and world are no longer noticed—not because one has withdrawn or dissociated from conditionally manifested phenomena, but because the Self-Abiding Divine Self-Recognition of all arising phenomena as modifications of the Divine Self-Condition has become so intense that the "Bright" Divine Conscious Light now Outshines all such phenomena.

Parama-Sapta-Na Sannyasin Circumstance—"Sapta Na Sannyasin" is a reference created by Avatar Adi Da Samraj to describe Himself as the seventh stage Reality-Guru, and also to describe His seventh stage (or Divinely Enlightened) devotees who are manifesting the most profound signs of the Divine Indifference phase of the seventh stage of life. ("Sapta" is Sanskrit for "seven", and "Na" is a reference to the Fijian Island of Naitauba, which is Avatar Adi Da's Principal Hermitage, the place where He Resides and where, as a general rule, His Sapta Na Sannyasin devotees will reside.) As the Unique Divine Avataric Revealer and Transmitter of the seventh stage Realization, Avatar Adi Da is the Parama-Sapta-Na Sannyasin (or "Supreme Sapta Na Sannyasin"). Because of His Unique Divine Avataric Function, the circumstance that must be provided for Him is one of profound freedom from any ordinary obligations, a circumstance in which He is absolutely Free to Manifest His Divine State.

"Perfect Knowledge"—See Appendix 3.

Perfectly Subjective—Avatar Adi Da uses this phrase to describe the True Divine Source (or "Subject") of the conditionally manifested worlds—as opposed to regarding the Acausal Divine as some sort of objective "Other". Thus, in the phrase "Perfectly Subjective", the word "Subjective" does not have the sense of "relating to the inward experience of an individual", but, rather, it has the sense of "Being Consciousness Itself, the True 'Subject' of all apparent experience".

"Perfect Practice"—The "Perfect Practice" is Avatar Adi Da's technical term for the discipline of the most mature demonstration of practice in the "Radical" Reality-Way of Adidam Ruchiradam. The "Perfect Practice" is practice in the domain of Consciousness Itself (as opposed to practice from the "point of view" of the body or the mind). The "Perfect Practice" unfolds in three phases, the third of which is Divine Enlightenment. This term is placed in quotation marks to indicate that His Divine Presence Avatar Adi Da uses it with the specific technical meaning described here.

"point of view"—By placing this phrase in quotation marks, Avatar Adi Da Samraj is communicating that, in Reality, every "point of view" is an illusion—because all ordinary viewpoints are founded in the false presumption of the separate existence of "I".

preliminary practice of "Perfect Knowledge" / preliminary "Perfect Knowledge" Listening-process of "Transcendental Root-Standing"—The practice that tacitly "locates" the "Perfect Knowledge" of Avatar Adi Da's State, for those who are yet identified with the faculties of the conditional body-mind. The Teachings and practice are "preliminary" because they are intended to lead to the fully mature practice of "Perfect Knowledge", which is established in the context of the "Perfect Practice" of Adidam Ruchiradam, when all identification with the conditional body and mind is transcended. The preliminary "Perfect Knowledge" practice is to be practiced in perpetual conjunction with the foundation practice of "radical" devotion and right life.

psycho-physical—A phrase which Avatar Adi Da Samraj uses to indicate that the human being is not a purely physical phenomenon, but a phenomenon with both physical and psychological/psychic dimensions. He also uses this description to characterize not only the human being but the world altogether.

"radical"—Derived from the Latin "radix" (meaning "root"), "radical" principally means "irreducible", "fundamental", or "relating to the origin". Thus, Avatar Adi Da defines "radical" as "at-the-root". Because Avatar Adi Da uses "radical" in this literal sense, it appears in quotation marks in His writings, in order to distinguish His usage from the common reference to an extreme (often political) view.

"Radical Conductivity"—A form of practice relative to the Energy-dimension of existence, given to prepared practitioners of Adidam in the "Perfect Practice", through confidential initiation by the Ruchira Sannyasin Order.

"radical" devotion—See Appendix 3.

"Radical Reality-Intuition"—Avatar Adi Da's term for the graceful "glimpses" of, or the uncaused Gift of resonance with, His Divine Reality-State, in the context of the preliminary "Perfect Knowledge" practice.

"Radical Self-Abiding"—The "Perfect Knowledge" dimension of Adidam as it is practiced in the context of the "Perfect Practice".

"Radical" Self-Manifestation of the "Thumbs"—See Appendix 5.

Ramana Maharshi—Ramana Maharshi (1879–1950) is regarded by many as the greatest Indian sage of the twentieth century. Following a spontaneous death-like event as a teenager, he abandoned home for a life of Spiritual practice. Eventually, an ashram was established around him at Tiruvannamalai in South India. Ramana Maharshi was a proponent of a form of "Self-enquiry" that involved tracing the thought of "I" (or separate existence) to its source.

recognition (devotional, of Ruchira Avatar Adi Da Samraj)—The foundation of the "Radical" Reality-Way of Adidam Ruchiradam is devotional recognition of Avatar Adi Da Samraj—or the direct and wordless "locating" and "knowing" of Avatar Adi Da as the "Bright", or Reality Itself, Appearing in bodily (human) Form.

renunciate—Practitioners of Adidam who enter the "Perfect Practice" necessarily do so as formal renunciates, because the process of the "Perfect Practice" is so profound and intensive that the individual's life must be entirely given over to that process.

right life / right-life obedience—See Appendix 3.

right side of the bodily apparent heart—See Appendix 2.

"root"-feeling of relatedness—The presumption of separation that is at the "root" of egoic existence.

Ruchira Sannyasin devotees—The Ruchira Sannyasin Order is the body of Avatar Adi Da's most exemplary devotees who have chosen to consecrate their lives utterly to Avatar Adi Da and the "Radical" Reality-Way of Adidam Ruchiradam—by embracing the life of formal and legal renunciation, in the circumstance of perpetual retreat. Avatar Adi Da has designated the Ruchira Sannyasin Order as the senior cultural authority within the gathering of His devotees—both during and after His physical Lifetime. Thus, it is the unique responsibility of the Ruchira Sannyasin Order to function both as the extension of Avatar Adi Da's sacred authority and as "Instrumentality", or the collective human "conduit", for His Transcendental Spiritual Blessing.

Ruchira Shaktipat—The "Bright" (Ruchira) Transcendental Spiritual Energy, or Transcendental Spiritual Power (Shakti), of Ruchira Avatar Adi Da Samraj.

sadhana—In Sanskrit, "sadhana" means "ego-transcending religious or Spiritual practice".

"Sadhana Years"—The period of time in Avatar Adi Da's early Life, starting when He most intensively began His Quest to recover the Truth of Existence (at Columbia University) in 1957 and ending with His Divine Re-Awakening in 1970. Avatar Adi Da's full description of His "Sadhana Years" is Given in *The Knee of Listening*.

The term "Sadhana Years" is placed in quotation marks to indicate that it is used by Avatar Adi Da in the "so to speak" sense. In this case, it indicates that, because of the Divine Avataric Nature of His Birth and Life, Avatar Adi Da's years of apparent "sadhana" were actually part of His Submission to humankind and preparation of the vehicle of His Body-Mind to Teach and Bless. Avatar Adi Da Samraj intentionally engaged His "Sadhana Years" as the Process of "Learning humankind". As the Avatarically Incarnate (and Inherently egoless) Divine Person, there was no other necessity for Him to engage any form of apparent "sadhana", because there was (in His Case) no egoity to be purified and transcended.

"Samraj Asana"—"Asana" is Sanskrit for bodily "posture" (or "pose"). Thus, "Samraj Asana" is "the 'pose' of devotion to Avatar Adi Da Samraj". "Samraj Asana" is a "pose" not of the physical body alone, but it is the structural disposition of the entire body-mind that Avatar Adi Da describes particularly in the Fourth Thorn of His "Four Thorns of Heart-Instruction". This "pose" is "healing" in the most profound sense, because it allows the release of "self"-contraction (including the release of the primal reactive emotions of fear, sorrow, anger, and un-love) and the reception of Avatar Adi Da's Transcendental Spiritual Divine Love-Bliss-Fullness.

"Samraj Yoga"—Avatar Adi Da defines "Samraj Yoga" in *The Dawn Horse Testament* as "The Total 'Perfect Practice' Yoga Of Utterly Transcending The First Six (or ego-Bound) Stages Of Life and (Thus and Thereby) Realizing The Only-By-Me Revealed and Given (and Divinely Enlightened, or Most Perfectly Divinely Awakened) Seventh Stage Of Life". Certain aspects of "Samraj Yoga" are described in *The Dawn Horse Testament*, but others are given only in initiation and instruction via the Ruchira Sannyasin Order of Adidam Ruchiradam, to those who are prepared to receive such instruction and initiation.

sannyasin—"Sannyasin" is a Sanskrit term for a renunciate who has formally relinquished all conventional social obligations in order to fully concentrate in intensive Spiritual practice.

Savikalpa Samadhi—See Appendix 5.

searchless Beholding (of Ruchira Avatar Adi Da Samraj)—The primary practice of the "Radical" Reality-Way of Adidam Ruchiradam, which begins after the foundation preparation is established. The practice of searchlessly Beholding Avatar Adi Da is the regarding of His bodily (human) Form, free of any seeking-effort, and the searchless "Locating" and "Knowing" of His Divine Transcendental Spiritual Self-Transmission.

Second Congregation—See Appendix 4.

Seeing—See **Listening, Hearing, Seeing**.

Self-Abiding Divine Self-Recognition—Divine Self-Recognition is the ego-transcending and world-transcending Intelligence of the Divine Acausal Self-Condition in relation to all conditional phenomena. The devotee of Avatar Adi Da who Realizes the seventh stage of life simply Abides as the Divine Conscious Light Itself, and he or she Freely Self-Recognizes (or inherently and instantly and most perfectly comprehends and perceives) all phenomena (including body, mind, conditional "self", and conditional "world") as transparent (or merely apparent), and unnecessary, and inherently non-binding modifications of the same "Bright" Conscious Light.

"self"-contraction—The fundamental presumption (and activity) of separation.

"self"-Enquiry—The practice of "self"-Enquiry (in the form "Avoiding relationship?") was spontaneously developed by Avatar Adi Da in the course of His own Ordeal of Divine Re-Awakening. Intense persistence in the "radical" discipline of this unique form of "self"-Enquiry led rapidly to Avatar Adi Da's Divine Re-Awakening (or Most Perfect Divine Self-Realization) in 1970.

Self-Existing and Self-Radiant—"Self-Existing" and "Self-Radiant" are terms describing the two fundamental aspects of the One Divine Person (or Reality)—Existence (or Being, or Consciousness) Itself, and Radiance (or Energy, or Light) Itself.

Self-Nature, Self-Condition, and Self-State (of Ruchira Avatar Adi Da Samraj / Reality Itself)—While pointing out that the presumption of an existent separate ego-"self" is an illusion, Avatar Adi Da Samraj uses this phrase to describe the True "Self" of everything that appears.

seventh stage—See Appendix 1.

Shaktipat Yoga—The process (Yoga) of receiving Spiritual Blessing-Transmission (Shaktipat).

Siddha-Grace / Siddha-Yoga—"Siddha" is Sanskrit for "a completed, fulfilled, or perfected one", or "one of perfect accomplishment, or power".

Avatar Adi Da uses "Siddha" to mean a Transmission-Master who is a Realizer (to some significant degree) of Reality Itself. "Siddha-Grace" is the Spiritual Transmission of the Siddha, and "Siddha-Yoga" is, literally, "the Yoga of the Perfected One[s]".

spinal line—See Appendix 2.

stages of life—See Appendix 1.

stations of the heart—See Appendix 2.

student-beginner—A student-beginner devotee of Avatar Adi Da Samraj is one who is formally acknowledged as demonstrating the impulse to practice the Reality-Way of Adidam in the most intensive manner—and who has also (as a Second Congregation devotee) firmly established the fundamental practice of "radical" devotion to Avatar Adi Da, fully adapted to all the right-life disciplines Given by Him, and seriously engaged the listening-study of His "Five Reality-Teachings". Student-beginner is the initial phase of practice in the First Congregation of Adidam. The transition into the First Congregation coincides with formal Initiation into the full preliminary Listening-practice of "Perfect Knowledge". See also Appendix 4.

"subject" / "subjective"—Avatar Adi Da consistently places the lower-case words "subject", "subjective", and so forth, in quotation marks. He does this in order to indicate that, in Reality Itself, there is no such thing as a "subject" that is separate from all potential "objects".

Swami (Baba) Muktananda—Swami Muktananda (1908–1982) was born in Mangalore, South India. Having left home at the age of fifteen, he wandered for many years, seeking the Divine Truth from sources all over India. Eventually, he came under the Spiritual Influence of Bhagavan Nityananda, whom he recognized as his Guru and in whose Spiritual Company he mastered Kundalini Yoga. Swami Muktananda served Avatar Adi Da as Guru during the period from 1968 to 1970. In the summer of 1969, during Avatar Adi Da's second visit to India, Swami Muktananda wrote a letter confirming Avatar Adi Da's attainment of "Yogic Liberation", and acknowledging His right to Teach others.

the "Thumbs"—See Appendix 5.

Transcendental Spiritual / Transcendental Spirituality—A principal description used by Avatar Adi Da Samraj of the unique nature of the process in His Company. As He describes in "Atma Nadi Shakti Yoga", all traditional forms of Spirituality are practiced on the "platform" of identification with the body-mind-"self". In contrast, the Transcendental

Spirituality of Adidam Ruchiradam is the Spiritual process that is founded in the transcending of identification with the body-mind-"self".

vertical dimension—See Appendix 2.

Vow / Eternal Vow—For a description of the Eternal Vow and responsibilities associated with the "Radical" Reality-Way of Adidam Ruchiradam, please see *The Reality-Way of Adidam* (forthcoming, The Dawn Horse Press, 2008).

Witness / Witness-Consciousness / Witness-Position—When Consciousness is free of identification with the body-mind, it stands in its natural "Position" as the conscious "Witness" of all that arises to and in and as the body-mind.

In the "Radical" Reality-Way of Adidam Ruchiradam, the stable realization of the "Witness-Position" is a gift from Avatar Adi Da, made possible by (and necessarily following upon) the reception of Avatar Adi Da's Transcendental Spiritual Blessing. The stable realization of the Witness-Position is a defining characteristic of the "Perfect Practice".

AN INVITATION

Become a Formal Devotee of His Divine Presence, The Divine Avataric World-Teacher, Ruchira Avatar Adi Da Samraj

Adidam is not a conventional "religion".
Adidam is not a conventional way of life.
Adidam is about the transcending of the ego-"I".

Adidam is about the Freedom of Divine Self-Realization.
Adidam is not based on mythology or belief.
Adidam is a Reality-practice.
Adidam is a "reality consideration", in which the various modes of egoity are directly transcended.

Adidam is a universally applicable Way of life.
Adidam is for those who will choose It, and whose hearts and intelligence fully respond to Me and My Offering.
Adidam is a Great Revelation, and It is to be freely and openly communicated to all.

—His Divine Presence
Ruchira Avatar Adi Da Samraj

In the depth of every being lies the inherent heart-impulse to be completely and utterly Free. In this book, you have been introduced to the Reality-Revelation of His Divine Presence Ruchira Avatar Adi Da Samraj, Who not only Speaks directly to this impulse, but Who Is That Freedom, Communicating Itself directly to you, and to all beings.

Ruchira Avatar Adi Da's Birth in 1939 was an intentional embrace of the human situation, for the sake of Revealing the Way of Divine Liberation to all and Offering the

Transcendental Spiritual Blessing that Awakens the Realization of Prior Freedom. His Divine Presence Adi Da Samraj is thus the fulfillment of the ancient intuitions of the "Avatar"—the One Who Appears in human Form, as a direct manifestation of Reality Itself.

In an unprecedented Teaching-Revelation process (beginning in 1972, and now complete), Ruchira Avatar Adi Da Samraj spoke for countless hours with those who recognized and devotionally responded to Him—always looking for them, as representatives of humanity, to ask all of their questions about God, Truth, Reality, and human life. In response, Avatar Adi Da Samraj created a vast body of Written and Spoken Teaching in which He Communicates in every detail the means for, and the signs of, ecstatic ego-transcending participation in the Direct Revelation of Reality Itself—As It Is, prior to body and mind and self and world. Thus, Avatar Adi Da created a new tradition based on His direct Avataric Revelation of Reality Itself: the "Radical" Reality-Way of Adidam Ruchiradam, which is the devotional and Transcendental Spiritual relationship to Him.

Ruchira Avatar Adi Da's True Function as Spiritual Master is not to teach or somehow magically "cause" Realization in His devotees. Rather, Avatar Adi Da's Function is to simply Be—As He Is, As the Divine Reality-State—and thus to make available to all beings the Direct Revelation of Reality Itself and the Means to Realize It. If you are moved to take up His Way, Avatar Adi Da Samraj invites you to enter into a direct and real devotional and Transcendental Spiritual relationship to Him.

To find His Divine Presence Ruchira Avatar Adi Da Samraj is to find the Very Heart of Reality—tangibly "known", prior to body and mind, as the Deepest Truth of Existence. This is the great mystery you are invited to discover. ■

I am not simply Speaking to those who are already My formal devotees. I am Speaking to everyone—literally.

I Meditate everybody. I Am everybody. And I am Speaking to everybody—but not to everybody as egos. I am Speaking to "everybody-all-at-once"—at the Heart, at the Place Where I Am. In that Place, there are no "differences". Where there are no "differences", people come to Me and are able to "Locate" Me and Commune with Me.

Adidam is not about egos. Adidam is not about an identity that comes through "belonging". Adidam is participation in the Divine.

You can participate in the Divine only in the Place of the Divine. The Divine Is a Place intrinsically without ego. The Divine is not a place you are "moving to". The Divine Is the Place Where you Are—Always Already.

The Divine Is Where there is no ego and no "other". Where there is an "other", there is no Real God, no Truth. Reality Itself Is Where there is no "other".

The Only Room That Is Is the Room in Which there is no "other", no "point of view"—but Only Real God, Only That Which Is Divine, Self-Existing, Self-Radiant, Indivisible, Acausal, Intrinsically egoless, Outshining all-and-All.

That is the "Temple" of Adidam. And That Is Where everybody Is—Always Already and egolessly.

—His Divine Presence
Ruchira Avatar Adi Da Samraj
May 31, 2008

On the following pages are a number of ways that you can choose to deepen your response to Avatar Adi Da and to consider becoming His formal devotee.

Visit the Adidam website: www.adidam.org

- **SEE AUDIO-VISUAL PRESENTATIONS** on the Divine Life and Transcendental Spiritual Revelation of Avatar Adi Da Samraj

- **LISTEN TO DISCOURSES** Given by Avatar Adi Da
  - Transcending egoic notions of God
  - Why Reality cannot be grasped by the mind
  - How the devotional relationship to Avatar Adi Da moves you beyond ego-bondage
  - The supreme process of Spiritual Transmission

- **READ QUOTATIONS** from the "Source-Texts" of Avatar Adi Da Samraj
  - Real (Acausal) God as the only Reality
  - The ancient practice of devotion to the Realizer
  - The two opposing life-strategies characteristic of the West and the East—and the way beyond both
  - The Prior Unity at the root of all that exists
  - The limits of scientific materialism
  - The true Way beyond all seeking
  - The esoteric structure of the human being
  - The real process of death and reincarnation
  - The nature of Divine Enlightenment

- **SUBSCRIBE** to the online *Adidam Revelation* magazine

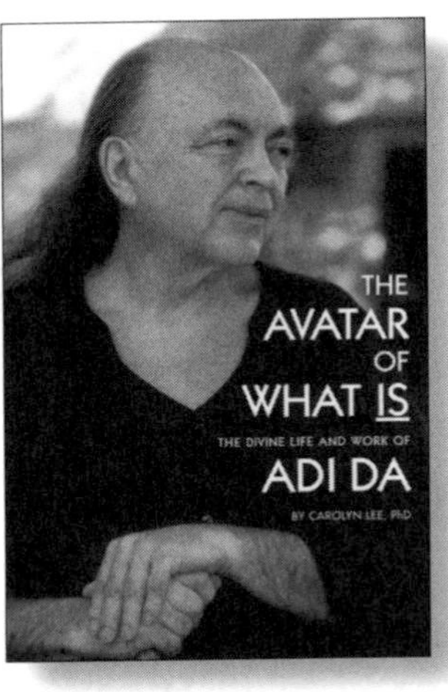

THE AVATAR OF WHAT IS

The Divine Life and Work of Adi Da

by Carolyn Lee, PhD

This new biography presents a summary overview of Avatar Adi Da's Life and Work from His Birth to the present time. From the foretelling of His Birth, through His years of "Learning humankind", to the more than thirty-five years of His unique Avataric Teaching-and-Blessing-Work, this is the extraordinary story of Avatar Adi Da's Divine Intervention in the world.

The Purpose of My bodily (human) Appearance here is the Divine Liberation of all of humankind—not merely the human beings of the East or the human beings of the West, but all human beings (and, indeed, all beings and things altogether).

—His Divine Presence Ruchira Avatar Adi Da Samraj

Avatar Adi Da's Divine Emergence marks a new chapter in epochal Spiritual History.

—**RICHARD GROSSINGER**
Author, *Planet Medicine, The Night Sky,* and *Embryogenesis*

The life and teaching of Avatar Adi Da are of profound and decisive spiritual significance at this critical moment in history.

—**BRYAN DESCHAMP**
Senior Adviser at the United Nations
High Commission for Refugees

There exists nowhere in the world today, among Christians, Jews, Muslims, Hindus, Buddhists, native tribalists, or any other groups, anyone who has so much to teach, or speaks with such authority, or is so important for understanding our situation. If we are willing to learn from him in every way, he is a Pole around which the world can get its bearings.

—**HENRY LEROY FINCH**
Author, *Wittgenstein—The Early Philosophy*
and *Wittgenstein—The Later Philosophy*

152 pp., **$12.95**

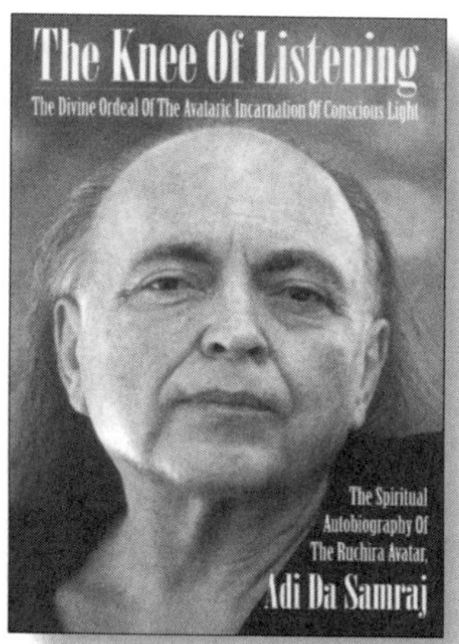

THE KNEE OF LISTENING

The Divine Ordeal Of The Avataric Incarnation Of Conscious Light

The Spiritual Autobiography of His Divine Presence Ruchira Avatar Adi Da Samraj

Born in 1939 on Long Island, New York, Avatar Adi Da Samraj describes His earliest Life as an existence of constant and unmitigated Spiritual "Brightness". His observation, still in infancy, that others did not live in this manner led Him to undertake an awesome quest—to discover why human beings suffer and how they can transcend that suffering. His quest led Him to a confrontation with the bleak despair of post-industrial Godlessness, to a minute examination of the workings of subjective awareness, to discipleship in a lineage of profound Yogis, to a period of intense Christian mysticism, and finally to a Re-Awakening to the perfect state of "Brightness" He had known at Birth.

In *The Knee of Listening*, Avatar Adi Da also reveals His own direct awareness of His "deeper-personality vehicles"—the beings whose lives were the direct antecedents (or the "pre-history") of His present human Lifetime—the great nineteenth-century Indian Realizers Sri Ramakrishna and Swami Vivekananda. Finally, Avatar Adi Da describes the series of profound transformational events that took place in the decades after His Divine Re-Awakening—each one a form of "Yogic death" for which there is no recorded precedent.

Altogether, *The Knee of Listening* is the unparalleled history of how the Divine Conscious Light has Incarnated in human form, in order to grant everyone the possibility of Ultimate Divine Liberation, Freedom, and Happiness.

The Knee of Listening *is without a doubt the most profound Spiritual autobiography of all time.*

—ROGER SAVOIE, PhD
Philosopher; translator; author, *La Vipère et le Lion: La Voie radicale de la Spiritualité*

822 pp., **$24.95**

MY "BRIGHT" WORD

by His Divine Presence
Ruchira Avatar Adi Da Samraj

New edition of the classic Spiritual Discourses originally published as *The Method of the Siddhas*

In these Talks from the early years of His Teaching-Work, Avatar Adi Da gives extraordinary Instruction on the foundation of True Spiritual life, covering topics such as the primary mechanism by which we are preventing the Realization of Truth, the means to overcome this mechanism, and the true function of the Spiritual Master in relation to the devotee.

In modern language, this volume teaches the ancient all-time trans-egoic truths. It transforms the student by paradox and by example. Consciousness, understanding, and finally the awakened Self are the rewards. What more can anyone want? —**ELMER GREEN, PhD**

Director Emeritus, Center for Applied Psychophysiology,
The Menninger Clinic

544 pp., **$24.95**

THE ANCIENT WALK-ABOUT WAY

The Core Esoteric Process of Real Spirituality and Its Perfect Fulfillment in the Way of Adidam

In this beautiful collection of essays, His Divine Presence Ruchira Avatar Adi Da begins with a foundation consideration of the purpose and principles of the ancient tradition of heart-response to the living Realizer; He then describes how to cultivate life-conditions that allow the being to enact its inherent heart-response to Living Truth; and, finally, He describes the unique Signs and Qualities of His Appearance and Offering, and of those who fully devotionally respond to Him.

Devotion to the Realizer is the ancient Way of true Spiritual life. Devotion to the Realizer is the "pre-civilization Way", which existed before any recorded history, during a time when human beings were, essentially, merely wandering all over the Earth. Devotion to the Realizer has always been the fundamental Means of human Spirituality.

—His Divine Presence Ruchira Avatar Adi Da Samraj

144 pp., **$12.95**

EASY DEATH

Spiritual Wisdom on the Ultimate Transcending of Death and Everything Else
by His Divine Presence
Ruchira Avatar Adi Da Samraj

This 2005 edition of *Easy Death* is thoroughly revised and updated with:

- Talks and essays from Avatar Adi Da on death and ultimate transcendence
- Accounts of profound events of Yogic death in Avatar Adi Da's own Life
- Stories of His Blessing in the death transitions of His devotees

. . . an exciting, stimulating, and thought-provoking book that adds immensely to the ever-increasing literature on the phenomena of life and death. But, more important, perhaps, it is a confirmation that a life filled with love instead of fear can lead to ultimately meaningful life and death. Thank you for this masterpiece.

—**ELISABETH KÜBLER-ROSS, MD**
Author, *On Death and Dying*

544 pp., **$24.95**

THE WORLD AS LIGHT

An Introduction to the Art of Adi Da Samraj
by Mei-Ling Israel

The condition of non-separateness—as the true nature of the human situation, and the true nature of Reality altogether—is the core of Avatar Adi Da's communication in His art. This generously illustrated book provides an overview of the massive body of highly distinctive artwork Avatar Adi Da Samraj has created over the past forty years—accompanied by key statements He has made on His own art and on the artistic process in general. Published on the occasion of Avatar Adi Da's collateral exhibition at the 52nd Biennale di Venezia (2007).

The living body always wants (with wanting need) to allow the Light of Perfect Reality into the "room". Assisting human beings to fulfill that impulse is what I work to do by every act of image-art.

—His Divine Presence Ruchira Avatar Adi Da Samraj

128 pp., with over 140 color and black-and-white illustrations, **$24.95**

THE WAY BEYOND EGO

Discourses Given by His Divine Presence
Ruchira Avatar Adi Da Samraj

The "self"-contraction, the knot, the action of egoity, must be transcended through recognition-response to That Which Transcends it. This is Given by direct Revelation, and not merely by philosophical propositions. It is not merely to be believed. It must be Revealed.

—His Divine Presence Ruchira Avatar Adi Da Samraj

In these Talks, Given in 2004 and 2005, Avatar Adi Da elucidates the essence, and the necessary foundation principles, of the Way in His Company. He makes clear that What He is Offering is not a way of self-applied techniques or self-generated experiences—rather, It is a Way of direct relationship to the Divine Person of Love-Bliss, Avatarically Appearing in and as His human Form.

2-CD set
Running times—Disc 1: 71 minutes; Disc 2: 39 minutes
$24.95

REALITY IS NOT WHAT YOU THINK

Yes, there are discrete forms, in some sense, but they are in Utter Unity, blended with one another absolutely, and in process eternally. . . .

What you perceive to be a universe, a cosmos of separate things, does not really exist.

—His Divine Presence Ruchira Avatar Adi Da Samraj

In this Discourse, Adi Da Samraj intensively considers the nature of egoity, clarifying that the sense of being a separate "something" is one's own activity. Because of this activity of separation—which He calls the "'self'-contraction"—the universe (and Reality altogether) is perceived to be a collection of separate "somethings". However, as Adi Da Samraj reveals, Reality is a Great Unity of Love-Bliss—and This can be realized when you become "a sacrifice in love, full of trust, Godward", and all fear (or the "self"-contraction) is transcended.

CD
Running time: 41 minutes
$14.95

THE ADIDAM REVELATION DISCOURSES on DVD

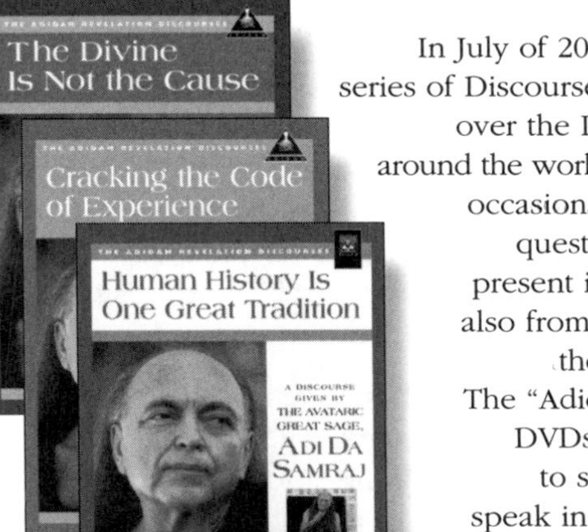

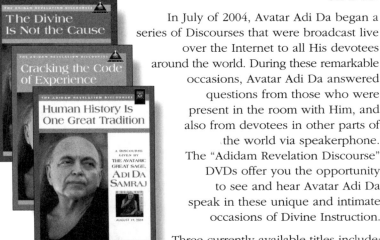

In July of 2004, Avatar Adi Da began a series of Discourses that were broadcast live over the Internet to all His devotees around the world. During these remarkable occasions, Avatar Adi Da answered questions from those who were present in the room with Him, and also from devotees in other parts of the world via speakerphone. The "Adidam Revelation Discourse" DVDs offer you the opportunity to see and hear Avatar Adi Da speak in these unique and intimate occasions of Divine Instruction.

Three currently available titles include:

THE DIVINE IS NOT THE CAUSE
Running time: 72 minutes. Includes subtitles in English, Spanish, French, German, Dutch, Finnish, Polish, Czech, Chinese, Japanese, and Hebrew.

CRACKING THE CODE OF EXPERIENCE
Running time: 86 minutes. Includes subtitles in English, Spanish, German, Dutch, Polish, Czech, Chinese, Japanese, and Hebrew.

HUMAN HISTORY IS ONE GREAT TRADITION
Running time: 74 minutes. Includes subtitles in English, Spanish, French, Italian, German, Dutch, Polish, Czech, Chinese, and Hebrew.

DVD, **$26.95** each

To order other books, tapes, CDs, DVDs, and videos by and about Avatar Adi Da, contact your local Adidam regional center, or contact

THE DAWN HORSE PRESS

1-877-770-0772 (from within North America)

1-707-928-6653 (from outside North America)

Or order online from: **www.dawnhorsepress.com**

Discover the Artistic Work of Avatar Adi Da Samraj

■ To find out about Avatar Adi Da's Literary and Theatrical Works, visit:
www.mummerybook.org

or contact the
First Room Theatre Guild:
12165 Shenandoah Road
Middletown, CA 95461
(707) 928-4853

■ For information about and examples of Avatar Adi Da's Visual Art, visit:

www.daplastique.com

www.adidabiennale.org

Support Avatar Adi Da's Work and the Reality-Way of Adidam

■ If you are moved to serve Avatar Adi Da's Work specifically through advocacy and/or financial patronage, please contact:

Advocacy
12180 Ridge Road
Middletown, CA 95461
phone: (707) 928-5267
email: adidam_advocacy@adidam.org

For young people: Join the Adidam Youth Fellowship

■ Young people under 21 can participate in the "Adidam Youth Fellowship"—either as a "friend" or practicing member. Adidam Youth Fellowship members participate in study programs, retreats, celebrations, and other events with other young people responding to Avatar Adi Da. To learn more about the Youth Fellowship, call or write:

Vision of Mulund Institute (VMI)
10336 Loch Lomond Road, PMB 146
Middletown, CA 95461
phone: (707) 928-6932
email: vmi@adidam.org
www.visionofmulund.org

Fear-No-More Zoo and Gardens

■ To learn more about Avatar Adi Da's regard for non-humans, visit:

www.fearnomorezoo.org

Or call or write:
Fear-No-More Zoo and Gardens
12040 North Seigler Road
Middletown, CA 95461, USA
phone: (707) 355-0638

Find out more about His Divine Presence Ruchira Avatar Adi Da Samraj and the Reality-Way of Adidam

■ Find out about courses, seminars, events, and retreats by calling the regional center nearest you.

AMERICAS
12040 N. Seigler Rd.
Middletown, CA
95461 USA
1-707-928-4936

EUROPE-AFRICA
Annendaalderweg 10
6105 AT Maria Hoop
The Netherlands
31 (0)20 468 1442

AUSTRALIA
P.O. Box 244
Kew 3101
Victoria
1800 ADIDAM
(1800-234-326)

THE UNITED KINGDOM
uk@adidam.org
0845-330-1008

PACIFIC-ASIA
12 Seibel Road
Henderson
Auckland 0614
New Zealand
64-9-838-9114

INDIA
F-168 Shree Love-Ananda Marg
Rampath, Shyam Nagar Extn.
Jaipur - 302 019, India
91 (141) 2293080

EMAIL: **correspondence@adidam.org**

■ Order books, tapes, CDs, DVDs, and videos by and about Ruchira Avatar Adi Da Samraj.

1-877-770-0772 (from within North America)
1-707-928-6653 (from outside North America)
order online: **www.dawnhorsepress.com**

■ Visit the Adidam website:

www.adidam.org

Discover more about Ruchira Avatar Adi Da Samraj and the Reality-Way of Adidam.